JESUS RETURNS THE WAY HE LEFT

JESUS RETURNS THE WAY HE LEFT

BASED ON HIS ASCENSION

Robert Parker

Robert's Trumpet
www.RobertsTrumpet.com

Copyright 2024 by Robert Parker

Published by Robert's Trumpet LLC
Winter Garden, FL

Seventh printing

ISBN: 979–8–9901137–0–1 (paperback)
ISBN: 979–8–9901137–1–8 (e–book)
ISBN: 979–8–9901137–2–5 (PDF)

Library of Congress Control Number: 2024915067

Graphic illustration book cover by Inflection Studios Design, 1469 W. Menlo Ave, Fresno, CA 93711. Https://Inflection-studios.com/graphic-design.

This book is written to provide eschatological insights into events, which may or may not happen in our lifetimes. It is sold with the understanding that neither the author nor publisher is engaged in rendering a professional service. If legal, medical, financial or other expert assistance is required, the services of a competent professional person should be sought.

To my loving parents

Table of Contents

List of Figures

Foreword

The pretribulation view, which is the most US popular premillennial rapture, has the church rapture before the seventieth week of Daniel with its massive amount of destruction. Some of these Protestant churches unfortunately make this part of their belief statement. This limits, and likely prevents, the church body from having an open discussion of other premillennial views. How can pretribulation rapture proponents be so adamant in their belief of future events? Scripturally they cannot prove it 100 percent, nor any rapture view, since Daniel 9:24–25 says that all prophecy will not be known until the end of the seventieth week of Daniel. This adamant view sets the church up for a future eschatological possible disaster.

Identifying and addressing risk is paramount in any business to survive and thrive. One way to quantify complex technical risks is to identify each known risk with a two-dimensional risk matrix. A matrix for each risk is made between of the likelihood of an event occurring using five increments (rare, unlikely, possible, likely, and most certain) versus the severity of five increments (insignificant, minor, moderate, major, and severe).

The severity of experiencing part or all of the seventieth week of Daniel, is unanimously acknowledged by scholars as severe. Daniel 12:1 describes the persecution "such as never has been." Yet, many pretribulation churches choose to ignore this recognized severe risk. They are assuming a low likelihood, high severity event, which would be like a hurricane, earthquake, or tsunami. If an identified risk could be mitigated, then a business would ideally resolve it as best as possible, else monitor it closely.

To mitigate this risk, all Bible-believing churches should remove their mandated pretribulation exegesis from their belief statements and be open to discussing other premillennial possibilities. Every other premillennial rapture theology has the church living through all to at least half of the seventieth week.

Beyond Prewrath provides a new premillennial view with the church entering the seventieth week and should be examined as to whether it has scriptural merit. This book is unique in that it goes further, to identify ways the church can mitigate the awful persecution that potentially awaits.

Abbreviations

1 Cor.	1 Corinthians
1 Sam.	1 Samuel
1 Thess.	1 Thessalonians
1 Tim.	1 Timothy
2 Cor.	2 Corinthians
2 Thess.	2 Thessalonians
AOD	Abomination of desolation
cf.	Compare
Dan.	Daniel
Day 1	Middle of the seventieth week of Daniel, also called midpoint
Day 1,260	End of the seventieth week of Daniel
Day 1,335	Start of the millennium when Jesus reigns for a thousand years
Deut.	Deuteronomy
Eph.	Ephesians
ESV	English Standard Version
Ex.	Exodus
Ezek.	Ezekiel
Gal.	Galations
Gen.	Genesis
Hab.	Habakkuk
Heb.	Hebrews
Isa.	Isaiah
Jer.	Jeremiah
Judg.	Judges
Lam.	Lamentations
Mal.	Malachi

Matt.	Matthew
Midpoint	Middle of the seventieth week of Daniel
Mt.	Mount
NASB	New American Standard Bible
NKJV	New King James Version
N. T.	New Testament
Num.	Numbers
Phil.	Philippians
Prov.	Proverbs
Ps.	Psalms
Rev.	Revelation
Rom.	Romans
T.	Trumpet blown
v.	Verse
vv.	Verses
Zech.	Zechariah
Zeph.	Zephaniah

Notes

Darkness and Light: Unless otherwise noted, *darkness* represents at least one twenty-four-hour cycle of no sunlight. The fifth blown trumpet in Revelation 9:2, 5 is one example of this *darkness* lasting five months. *Light* is used to represent a normal twenty-four-hour cycle of daytime and nighttime.

Middle/End of Seventieth Week: The middle of the seventieth week of Daniel is called Day 1 or midpoint since that is when the fifth opened seal of great tribulation and Jacob's trouble begin. This is representative of the prophet Daniel's counting in Daniel 12:11–12. The end of the seventieth week is called Day 1,260.

Sheep: Unless otherwise noted, the sheep are a reference to those from the sheep and goat judgment. Their rapture in Revelation 16:18 theophany is based only on at least one of Matthew 25:35–40 six acts of kindness to "my (Jesus) brothers."

Introduction

BOOK OVERVIEW

This book provides many eschatological insights, based on the *beyond prewrath* and other understandings, as summarized below.

I. BEYOND PREWRATH EXEGESIS

The new premillennial *beyond prewrath* rapture exegesis can be summarized with seven supporting themes, which is discussed in chapters 1 to 6. There are three dispensational (not partial) raptures: church-elect (Rev. 8:5), Israel (Rev. 11:19), and the works-based "sheep" (Rev. 16:18). Jesus returns from heaven to earth at the midpoint with His resurrected saints.

FIRST EXEGESIS, JESUS RETURNS THE WAY HE LEFT

Jesus must return the way he left as supported with Acts 1:9–11. Verse 12 says Jesus ascended from the Mt. of Olives and must therefore return there as described in Zechariah 14:4. The chronological parallel of fleeing to/my mountain in Zechariah 14:5 and Matthew 24:16 provide more support. The previous verse 15 with the abomination of desolation ties it to the midpoint with Daniel 9:27.

SECOND, GATHERINGS AND DAYS OF THE LORD

Chapter 1 proposes at least two different chronological pairs of gatherings and days of the Lord and not the commonly held one pair. The first pair, 2 Thessalonians 2:1 gathering and 2:3 day of the Lord, is associated with the midpoint coming of Jesus from heaven to the ground at the Mt. of Olives (Dan. 9:27; Zech. 14:1–5; Matt. 24:15–17, 27) with the gathering of those in the city of David (Isa. 33:17; Zech. 14:5; Matt. 24:16–17). The second pair is associated with the elect rapture after the great tribulation with the gathering in the sky (1 Thess. 4:17; Rev. 1:7) and the same day "day of the Lord" in Revelation 8:7.[1]

THIRD, WICKED DESTROYED WITH FIRE

No other premillennial rapture view can point to Scripture closely linking their rapture event with the day of the Lord, characterized by fire and death. In Revelation 8:5 theophany, beyond prewrath identifies the rapture (day of Christ) of the elect, followed in verse 7 by the same day "day of the Lord," echoing Jesus's prophecy in Luke 17:26–30 concerning Noah and Lot. Secondly, this close sequence (Rev. 8:5 and 8:7) prevents the interpretation that the events depicted by the opened seals overlap with those of the blown trumpets.

FOURTH, FOUR UNIQUE THEOPHANIES

The three-time unique theophany phrase "peals of thunder, rumblings, flashes of lightning, and an earthquake" is only found in Revelation 8:5 (seventh opened seal), 11:19 (seventh blown trumpet), and 16:18 (seventh poured bowl). An earlier theophany, except for the earthquake, can only be found in Revelation 4:5–11 which is emanating from the heavenly throne with God.

Each earthly theophany is proposed to be the Lord's presence, which represents a chronologically different dispensational rapture. The first is for the church, second is for Israel, and the third is for the works-based sheep (Matt. 25:35–36) from the sheep and goat judgment. The first two faith-based groups represent the bride of Christ who alone attend the béma (Rev. 11:18).

---

1   The unknown day and hour mentioned in Matthew 24:36–39 pertains to the separation of the righteous from God's wrath, as exemplified by Lot and Noah. Nowhere does Scripture indicate that Jesus's second return, from heaven to earth, will occur simultaneously with this separation (rapture). Instead, Jesus's second return will be presented as a series of events, just as His first return was. For further details, see Chapter 5, First Prewrath Problem.

FIFTH, NEED TO ACCOUNT FOR ISRAEL'S SAFETY

Beyond prewrath accounts for Israel's remnant. Consider what happens when the remnant's 1,260 days (Rev. 12:14) of protection end while the Antichrist is still on the earth? There must be a unique rapture for spiritually saved Israel on earth to take them to the béma (Rev. 11:18), which is in Revelation 11:19 theophany represented as the last verse of the seventh blown trumpet on Day 1,260. This is exactly when their decreed seventieth week on earth ends (Dan. 9:24–25).

SIXTH, WORKS-BASED SHEEP REIGNED OVER

The works-based sheep are accounted for, from the sheep and goat judgment, who must later inherit their kingdom when Christ reigns during the millennial kingdom (Matt. 25:33–34). It is not reasonable for the bride of Christ to attend the béma, marriage supper, Armageddon battle with Jesus, but then during the millennium be subjects to their brothers (Rev. 20:4–5). The sheep must be deduced to be the subjects being reigned over. The sheep's rapture is based on works (Matt. 25:35–36) and not faith in Jesus. The sheep appear to be the wedding guests who are invited to the marriage supper (Matt. 22:1–10; Rev. 19:9–10).

The sheep will live long lives with a physical death, though their children could live to the end of the millennium. A rapture by itself, as with the sheep, does not necessarily represent receiving an imperishable body. Consider the Apostle Philip who was raptured to a different location on earth (Acts 8:34–40), though later had a physical death.

SEVENTH, CHRONOLOGY

Chapter 6 discusses seven chronological reasons. The first six explain why Revelation chapters 6 to 8 are not strictly chronological. The seventh reason involves Jesus's coming in Matthew 24:27 before verse 29, with verse 29 being chronologically parallel to Revelation 6:12. Verse 12 explicitly identifies the sixth seal as being opened when there is 24 hour darkness, which is not present during the fifth seal. The fifth opened seal begins with the abomination of desolation at the midpoint (Dan. 9:27; Matt. 24:15). Therefore, Jesus's coming aligns with the earlier fifth opened seal, as depicted in figure 13 at the midpoint.

The gathering described in Matthew 24:30–31 occurs after the identified sixth opened seal of verse 29. Verses 30–31 must be a consequence of an earthly rapture, where the elect receive imperishable bodies and then ascend to meet Jesus in the sky (1 Thess. 4:17; Rev. 1:7). This deduction is supported by the need for planting and building (Luke 17:26–30), daytime events that are not practical during the extended 24-hour darkness of the sixth seal.

II. CHAPTERS 7 TO 12

These chapters explore various topics including the three battles of Ezekiel 38 and 39, Israel's three-part journey during the second half of the seventieth week, the lack of overlap among seals and trumpets, the Antichrist and the restrainer, endurance and faith, and definitions related to the beyond prewrath perspective.

III. FIFTH AND SIXTH PRINTING CHANGES

This fifth print corrects the resurrection from concurrent Revelation 8:5 and 11:19 dispensational raptures to the midpoint with Jesus second coming from heaven to earth. The sixth print removes the reference to the first resurrection (fifth print), though only generally discussions the resurrection. The label of "great eschatological theophany" was changed to "great dispensational theophany." An effort was made in chapter 3 to harmonize the works-based (Matt. 25:34–36) and the faith-based eternal life sheep (v. 46b).

Chapter 1

Jesus's Return to the Mt. of Olives

INTRODUCTION

Jesus must return the same way he left as according to Acts 1:9–11. Verse 12 says he ascended into heaven *from the Mt. of Olives*; therefore, it seems he must return there. Figure 1 chronologically parallel Scriptures support Jesus coming (Matt. 24:27, Greek noun *parousia*) from heaven to earth at the midpoint of the seventieth week of Daniel (Dan. 9:27; Matt. 24:15). Then there is a continued presence, as the definition of parousia implies. The beyond prewrath rapture of the elect does not occur the day of Jesus coming from heaven to earth at this midpoint, as with the midtribulation. The elect rapture is proposed to happen later after the great tribulation ends though before the first blown trumpet of Revelation 8:7 with its fire and death as Jesus's prophecy in Luke 17:28–30.

This author proposes that there is more than one eschatological pair of a gathering and a day of the Lord. One of the pairs, the second, must be associated with a rapture to fulfill Jesus's prophesy as in the days of Lot and Noah. That is, one of the gatherings, which is in the sky, would need to be the consequence of the earthly elect rapture with its same day "day of the Lord."

The first pair is proposed to be at the midpoint when Jesus returns the way he left to the Mt. of Olives (Zech. 14:1–5; Acts 1:12) with those nearby on their housetops (Matt. 24:17). This first gathering of those on their housetops and Jesus's feet on the Mt. of Olives would both be on the ground, which is different from the later second gathering when Jesus and the elect are in the sky. The 2 Thessalonians 2:1–4 pair cannot be directly identified to be associated with the elect rapture since it does not have the word rapture (Greek *harpazó*) or meeting location of sky or heaven. It is proposed to occur in the first pair.

Satan's forced parousia in Revelation 12:7–12 (cf. Luke 10:18) will also occur at the midpoint when he is thrown out of heaven to earth. This begins an unparalleled time of persecution, which is the great tribulation (Matt. 24:21) and Jacob's trouble (Jer. 30:7; Dan. 12:1; Matt. 24:16–20). Moments before the trouble begins, there is a proposed gathering of those on their Jerusalem housetops with Jesus on or near the Mt. of Olives. That same

Jewish day Israel is attacked by Gog and the Jewish remnant who flee to the east, some say to Petra, will be granted persecution relief for three and a half years. Those in Israel who do not flee will have extreme persecution and possibly death.

> And when he had said these things, as they were looking on, he was lifted up, and a cloud took him out of their sight. And while they were gazing into heaven (sky) as he went, behold, two men stood by them in white robes, and said, "Men of Galilee, why do you stand looking into heaven? *This Jesus,* who was taken up from you into heaven, *will come in the same way as you saw him go into heaven.* Then they returned to Jerusalem *from the mount called Olivet,* which is near Jerusalem, a Sabbath day's journey away." (Acts 1:9–12, emphasis added)

FIGURE 1: JESUS RETURNS THE WAY HE LEFT

Daniel/Acts	Matthew/Acts	Isaiah/Zechariah/2 Thessalonians
		Day of the Lord (Zech. 14:1)
Jesus to return the way he left (Acts 1:9–11)	Jesus ascended into heaven from Mt. of Olives (Acts 1:12)	His feet on the Mt. of Olives (Zech. 14:4)
		Our gathering (2 Thess. 2:1) See King in his beauty (Isa. 33:17)
	Those in Judea flee to the mountains (Matt. 24:16)	Flee to the valley of my mountains for Judah (Uzziah) (Zech. 14:5)
Abomination of desolation at midpoint (Dan. 9:27)	Abomination of desolation as with Daniel (Matt. 24:15)	

FIGURE 1 CONNECTING SCRIPTURE THEMES

The Scriptures shown in figure 1 supports Jesus's parousia (Acts 1:9–11) at the midpoint (Dan. 9:27) with a day of the Lord (Zech. 14:1, 5) and a gathering (2 Thess. 2:1; Isa. 22:1), though does not include a rapture. Starting with Acts 1:9–11, the arrows in the figure above will lead the reader from common Scripture to common Scripture, as described below.

1) Acts 1:9–11 to 1:12: Jesus must return the way he left. These two sets of Scriptures are sequential and of the same thought.

2) Acts 1:12 to Zechariah 14:4: The geographically unique Mt. of Olives location and Jesus connects these two Scriptures. The Mt. of Olives has never been split and a wide valley formed, as discussed in Zechariah 14:4; therefore, it is a future prophetic Scripture.

3) Zechariah 14:1–5: These five Scripture verses in the third column are sequential and of the same thought. Verse 1 has it as a day of the Lord, which is later supported at the midpoint with Daniel 9:27.

4) 2 Thessalonians 2:1 and Isaiah 33:17: Zechariah 14:1, 5 support a day of the Lord associated with Jesus second coming, though no rapture word is present. Jesus's feet are on the ground, rather than in the sky (Matt. 24:30–31; Rev. 1:7), point to this different interpretation. Matthew 24:17 has those on their Judea (current Israel) nearby housetops, which then opens the door that this midpoint, Jesus's parousia, could be the first gathering.

5) Zechariah 14:5 to Matthew 24:16: Nowhere else in Scripture is there found both *flee* and *to the/my mountains* providing a strong two word thought for thought fit. Zechariah 14:5 and Matthew 24:16, with the same Judah/Judea location, provides a third exegetical word.

6) Matthew 24:15 and 16: These two Scriptures are sequential and of the same thought.

7) Matthew 24:15 to Daniel 9:27: Both Scriptures discuss the abomination of desolation, which the prophet Daniel time stamps to the midpoint.

> And you shall *flee to the valley of my mountains*, for the valley of the mountains shall reach to Azal. And you shall flee as you fled from the earthquake in the days of Uzziah king of *Judah*. Then the Lord my God will come, and all the holy ones with him. (Zech. 14:5, emphasis added)

Then let *those who are in Judea flee to the mountains*. (Matt. 24:16, emphasis added)

THREE CONCLUSIONS OF FIGURE 1

First, Jesus's parousia from heaven to earth occurs at the midpoint. Figure 1 chronologically linked Scriptures supported Jesus's coming of Acts 1:9–11 with the midpoint of Daniel 9:27.

Second, this midpoint is not representative of a rapture of the elect since Matthew 24:21–28 and Revelation 7:9–17 have the church living through the great tribulation's fifth opened seal.

Third, Jesus's return to the Mt. of Olives (Acts 1:11; Zech. 14:4) is likely a gathering with those nearby on their present-day Israel housetops (Matt. 24:16–17) followed that day with a day of the Lord (Zech. 14:1, 5). The duration of the gathering and day of the Lord does not seem to exceed a day, since there is an urgency to flee their housetops with the same day abomination of desolation and the later light in the evening (Zech. 14:6).

Zechariah 14:4–5, 10 describes a wide valley which extends for many miles though "Jerusalem shall remain aloft on its site." Therefore, those in Jerusalem on their housetops would seem to be mainly, if not only, those viewing the Mt. of Olives. This close viewing of about a mile or so should be considered a gathering with Jesus.

FIGURE 2 – 2 THESSALONIANS FOCUS

Figure 2 below is another perspective of the multi-faceted events occurring at the midpoint which are hinged on the first two chapters of 2 Thessalonians. Each row of the figure provides a chronological sequential view of events focused on the midpoint with the first rows occurring first and later rows occurring later. Each Scripture row represents the same event. Several of these event rows are expected to chronologically overlap.

Now concerning the coming of our Lord Jesus Christ and our being gathered together to him, we ask you, brothers, not to be quickly shaken in mind or alarmed, either by a spirit or a spoken word, or a letter seeming to be from us, to the effect that the day of the Lord has come. Let no one deceive you in any way. For that day will not come, unless the rebellion comes first, and the man of lawlessness is revealed, the son of destruction, who opposes and exalts himself against every so-called god or object of worship, so that he takes his seat in the temple of God, proclaiming himself to be God. (2 Thess. 2:1–4)

FIGURE 2: MIDPOINT EVENTS: FOCUS ON 2 THESSALONIANS

Daniel / Zechariah	Matthew 24	Revelation/Isaiah	2 Thessalonians
	Fourth seal of tribulation (v. 9)		Church rebellion (2:3a)
	Gospel proclaimed world-wide (v. 14)	Angel proclamation (Rev. 14:6–7)	
Abomination of desolation at midpoint (Dan. 9:27)	Temple abomination of desolation (v. 15)	Satan thrown out of heaven (Rev. 12:7–12)	Man of lawlessness revealed in the temple (2:3–4)
His feet on the Mt. of Olives (Zech. 14:4)	On their housetops (v. 17). Coming of Jesus (v. 27)	Behold the King (Isa. 33:17)	Marveled at (1:10). Gathered to him (2:1b)
Day of the Lord (Zech. 14:1)			Day of the Lord (2:1a)
Flee to the valley of my mountains (Zech. 14:5)	Those in Judea flee to the mountains (v. 16)	Israel remnant nourished 3.5 years (Rev. 12:14)	Relief to those afflicted (1:7)

FIGURE 2, FIRST ROW: CHURCH REBELLION

Figure 1 previous analysis provided support that the first gathering and first day of the Lord is at the midpoint, not for a rapture. Before this day of the Lord in 2 Thessalonians 2:1–3, it says a rebellion (Greek *apostasía*) occurs for those who have been enlightened (Heb. 6:4–6). Prior to the midpoint is the fourth opened seal with its tribulation (Matt. 24:9–14; Rev. 6:7–8), which is where the church spiritual falling away is expected to start.

FIGURE 2, SECOND ROW: GOSPEL PREACHED

Shortly before Jesus's ascension into heaven, he gave us the Matthew 28:16–20 Great Commission. The church has made significant advancements in fulfilling this, though it is doubtful it will ever quite fulfill it. This prophecy seems to be fulfilled in Matthew 24:14 with the help of the chronologically parallel first angel proclamation of Revelation 14:6–7. Matthew 24:14 seems to be chronologically parallel to this since it is located just before the midpoint abomination of desolation in verse 15.

> And this gospel of the kingdom will be proclaimed throughout the whole world as a testimony to all nations, and then the end will come. (Matt. 24:14)

> Then I saw another angel flying directly overhead, with an eternal gospel to proclaim to those who dwell on earth, to every nation and tribe and language and people. And he said with a loud voice, "Fear God and give him glory, because the hour of his judgment has come, and worship him who made heaven and earth, the sea and the springs of water." (Rev. 14:6–7)

The Great Commission fulfillment with the first angel proclamation then frees the church to focus on their families to endure (Matt. 24:13) a time of great persecution. For the church to try to witness to those who have been previously enlightened, though have now fallen away, seems fruitless in light of Hebrews 6:4–6. This seems representative of 2 Thessalonians 2:11, which says the wicked will have a strong delusion from God. They are still physically alive on earth, though spiritually they have committed themselves to eternity in hell (Rev. 14:9–11). In a sense, they are the walking dead. Matthew 12:32 describes this eternal sin as blasphemy of the Holy Spirit.

For it is impossible, in the case of those who have once been enlightened, who have tasted the heavenly gift, and have shared in the Holy Spirit, and have tasted the goodness of the word of God and the powers of the age to come, and then have fallen away, to restore them again to repentance, since they are crucifying once again the Son of God to their own harm and holding him up to contempt. (Heb. 6:4–6)

And whoever speaks a word against the Son of Man will be forgiven, but whoever speaks against the Holy Spirit will not be forgiven, either in this age or in the age to come. (Matt. 12:32)

FIGURE 2, THIRD ROW: ABOMINATION THEN FLEE

The command to flee in Matthew 24:16 is just after verse 15, which says, "So when you see the abomination of desolation spoken of by the prophet Daniel, standing in the holy place (let the reader understand)." This is a direct reference to Daniel 9:27, which has this abomination at the midpoint.

And he shall make a strong covenant with many for one week, and for *half of the week* (midpoint) he shall put an end to sacrifice and offering. And on the *wing of abominations shall come one who makes desolate*, until the decreed end is poured out on the desolator. (Dan. 9:27, emphasis added)

Another way to identify 2 Thessalonians 2 at the midpoint is based on knowing when the Daniel 9:27 treaty is made strong by the prince (little horn). When this becomes public, all one needs to do is add half a prophetic week (one thousand two hundred and sixty days) to its signing to determine when this midpoint would begin. It is unclear whether the prince will make the treaty strong on the day it is signed or whether this will occur before or after. Some may say that the signing of the seven-year covenant would not make international news. For this to be kept a secret would be very doubtful since it would cause Israel and those countries signing it to think the other party was not going to fulfill the agreement.

FIGURE 2, FOURTH ROW: GATHERING LOCATION

Both 2 Thessalonians 1:10 and 2:1 discuss Jesus's parousia. What is unique in 2 Thessalonians 1 is that verse 10 says, "When he comes on that day to be glorified in his saints, and to be marveled at among all who have believed, because our testimony to you was believed." To be *marveled at* does not by itself represent a rapture. This seems reflective of *to behold the King in his beauty* (Isa. 33:17) and being gathered to him (2 Thess. 2:1; cf. Matt. 24:17). There is no indication of a multitude rejoicing in heaven in 2 Thessalonians 1 or 2, nor can the Greek word harpazó for rapture be found here. It is a different event than with Revelation 7:9–17, which is a consequence of a rapture of those who lived through the fifth opened seal of the great tribulation. Those on their Jerusalem housetops are expected to see Jesus, which is considered a gathering.

For those in the city of David, that is Jerusalem, Isaiah seems to have this gathering to begin when they are alerted in prayer inside their houses with the 22:1 "oracle concerning the valley of vision." It says, "What do you mean that you have gone up, all of you, to the housetops?" Although the Jewish people on their Jerusalem housetops are only about a mile or two from the Mt. of Olives, it is still considered close enough for a gathering place before they flee. The Kidron Valley between the two locations has no structures blocking their view. This then forms an ideal location for a gathering when shortly after Jesus's feet set down on the Mt. of Olives. Then a major earthquake will split the Mt. of Olives in two creating the wide valley described in Zechariah 14:4 where they will likely see afar to the east the mountains in present-day Jordan (Zech. 14:5).

FIGURE 2, FIFTH ROW: DAY OF THE LORD

In 2 Thessalonians 2:1, it has both a day of the Lord and a gathering, although there is no explicit mention of the rapture (Greek *harpazó*) anywhere in the chapter. Prewrath proponents assert that this gathering mentioned in 2 Thessalonians 2 is in the sky, representative of a deduced rapture event. However, it is worth noting that earlier analysis disputes the assumption of only one gathering with Jesus. Additionally, prewrath proponents claim there is only one eschatological day of the Lord, which will be further disputed in the next chapter.

Considering the apostle Paul's writing in 2 Thessalonians 2, it is notable that he didn't explicitly state that they wouldn't enter the eschatological day of the Lord. Instead, he emphasized that two events must occur before they are gathered together. These precursor events are the falling away of the church and the revealing of the man of lawlessness. The timing of this revelation is crucial as it best aligns with placing the day of the Lord mentioned in verse 1 at the midpoint.

In this context, the prince (little horn), associated with the midpoint abomination of desolation at the new temple or possibly tabernacle, should be sufficient to reveal his identity. The consequence of this event should be expected to disrupt the twice daily priestly temple sacrifices and cause them to flee, starting Jacob's trouble. This trampling of the temple has a duration of 1,260 days (Rev. 11:1–2), which ends when the seventieth week is fulfilled for the Jewish people.

FIGURE 2, LAST ROW: RELIEF FROM PERSECUTION

2 Thessalonians 1:7 has "relief to you who are afflicted." This affliction likely starts in the fourth opened seal of tribulation (Matt. 24:9–14; Rev. 6:7–8). The earlier four rows provide support that the parousia of Jesus from heaven to earth is at the midpoint when those who are on their housetops gathered behold King Jesus. It is when the abomination of desolation occurs that those in Judea are commanded to flee to the valley of the mountain. This mountain is the Mt. of Olives, which Jesus will return to as he left.

Those in Judea are commanded to flee in Matthew 24:15–20, as discussed in figure 1. This figure supports those in Judea who flee to the/my valley of the mountains as occurring at the midpoint with the abomination of desolation. It also supports the consequence of this command *to flee* in Matthew 24:15–20 and Zechariah 14:5 is chronologically parallel to Revelation 12:13–16 where Satan is pursuing the woman (Israel's remnant). It is only when Satan gives up the chase that he then makes war against "those who keep the commandments of God and hold to the testimony of Jesus (church)" in Revelation 12:17, which is chronologically parallel to the start of Jacob's (Israel's) trouble in Matthew 24:15–20 followed by the world's great tribulation in Matthew 24:21–26.

Therefore, this midpoint *relief* must be interpreted for the Jewish remnant in Israel when they immediately flee and are then nourished and protected for three and a half years (Rev. 12:13–16; cf. Ps. 4:1). 2 Thessalonians 1:7 *relief* cannot be applicable to the elect who must now live through the great tribulation, though it will be cut short for them.

NUMERICALLY VISUALIZE TO CUT SHORT

To help numerically visualize the fifth opened seal great tribulation being cut short, though the second half of the seventieth week duration remaining the same, consider the following hypothetical example. Say the Lord cuts short the great tribulation from a duration of thirty months. Also, hypothetically he intended the first four blown trumpets and the last two to have a duration of seventeen months. We already know the fifth blown trumpet is five months long in Revelation 9:5, so that is not going to change. There are a total of forty-two prophetic months in the second half of the prophetic week.

Say the Lord cut short the great tribulation by twelve months, then it becomes eighteen months (30 − 12 = 18). Then, under this hypothesis, the duration of the first four blown trumpets would have to increase by these twelve months to twenty-nine months (17 + 12 = 29). These changes represent the great tribulation being cut short, though they would still fulfill the Daniel 9:24–25 prophecy duration of the seventieth week of Daniel having a prophetic week. Almost all premillennial scholars, if not all, recognize that a prophetic week is a duration of seven years, where a year has three hundred and sixty days, and a month has thirty days.

JESUS'S RETURN IS NOT A RAPTURE EVENT

The Israel remnant being commanded to flee and the church living through the great tribulation can in no way be interpreted as a rapture the day Jesus returns from heaven to earth. Revelation 7:13–14 confirms this later elect rapture chronology since it describes those who lived through the great tribulation as rejoicing in heaven.

FLEE TO THE MOUNTAINS AND PETRA

To flee at the midpoint would be from the temple mount with its joyous new temple celebration and those on their housetops in the city of David with the gathering. This rejoicing will have started several days earlier with the Passover as proposed in *Jesus's Return based on the Feasts of the Lord*. It also proposes the two witnesses arriving on this Passover when the temple sacrifices would begin again after almost two thousand years. If so, then the temple mount would still be crowded with Jewish people celebrating. The vast majority of Jewish people have never been on the temple mount, even though the Israel Defense Force took control of it in 1967. Having this opportunity to walk on the temple mount with the new temple could draw hundreds of thousands of people.

The fleeing direction of Matthew 24:16 would be from the temple mount and toward where the Mt. of Olives once was, which is an eastward direction. This general direction is supported by many scholars who believe the Israel remnant flees to Petra, which is located on the other side of the Dead Sea from Israel, part of present-day Jordan. Petra is popular with Christian tours and now recognizable from the iconic 1989 movie *Indiana Jones and the Last Crusade*. This author has a different perspective as to where they will flee.

The command in Zechariah 14:5 to "flee to the valley of my mountains" seems to occur as a result of Jesus returning to the Mt. of Olives, the earthquake, and those in Jerusalem fleeing toward where it once was. The Mt. of Olives becoming part of a valley becomes part of the wide plain (vv. 4, 10), and then water flowing (v. 8) eastward and westward from the temple mount area. During the millennium, the debris from the mountain on the east side of the temple mount would be continued carried downhill by the year-round flowing river (Ezek. 47:1–12) through its newly formed valley to the Dead Sea.

In Revelation 12:15, Satan attempts to destroy the woman (a remnant of Israel) with a large body of flowing water, but she manages to flee. Daniel 9:26 mentions that "its end shall come with a flood." The preceding verse describes the chronologically earlier second temple being built when there was a moat of water surrounding the historic Jerusalem city. The flowing living water in Zechariah 14:8 (cf. Ezek. 47:1–12) at or just before the midpoint could create another moat of water during these troubled times.

When considered together, these passages suggest a literal, localized flood originating from the Zechariah 14:4 Mt. of Olives splitting (analogous to a dam wall collapsing) then water in the moat flowing towards the Dead Sea, rather than merely a metaphor for destruction. Some of the moat water could flow west toward the Mediterranean Sea. Satan's intent is to annihilate the Jewish people, yet a remnant is swept away to safety, where the earth provides protection and sustenance for 1,260 days (Rev. 12:13–16).

The flash flood and the ongoing river flowing eastward from the former Mt. of Olives could, during the millennium, gradually transport this earthen mound towards the Dead Sea. This scenario would fulfill the prophecy in Mark 11:20–25, which emphasizes the power of faith.

Truly, I say to you, whoever says to *this mountain* (Mt. of Olives), 'Be taken up and thrown into the sea,' and does not doubt in his heart, but believes that what he says will come to pass, it will be done for him. (Mark 11:23, emphasis added)

LIVING WATER AND DEAD SEA CAVERNS

Petra has rock carved architecture with sandstone cliffs, but it has no deep cavities for housing a multitude of Jewish people. Consider how the Israel remnant would be nourished and protected from Satan for three and a half years (Rev. 12:13–16). They must be provided with daily access to fresh water, food, and protection during the second half of the seventieth week.

Their nourishment could come from the aquatic animal life of Zechariah 14:8 Jerusalem source of living waters, which appears to begin flowing at the midpoint from Jerusalem to the eastward and westward seas. Ezekiel 47:1–12 supports a later only eastward year-round river flowing in the millennium. Verses 9–10 indicate the abundant number of fish, which could provide their nourishment. Petra could not provide this since it is located on the other side of the Dead Sea. That is, water can only flow down from the Jerusalem temple mount (2,428 feet) to the Dead Sea (-1,412 feet), though not then higher from the Dead Sea to Petra (2,657 feet).

The eastward flowing fresh water could then enter the salt caverns before emptying into the Dead Sea. These caverns were created over the last few decades as the Dead Sea elevation receded. This exposed a labyrinth of caverns which are located on the northwestern side of the Dead Sea. At least one of these extends for a few miles and could provide safety for hundreds if not thousands of people. Later as the trumpet and bowl judgments occur with the waters of the earth drying up or becoming polluted with blood (Rev. 8:10–11, 16:4–7, 12), these two Jerusalem rivers could be the only source of fresh water on earth. This may be a large part of why the later Jehoshaphat and Armageddon battles are fought in Israel.

OTHER POSSIBLE ATTRIBUTES OF JESUS'S RETURN

The following are some other possible attributes of Jesus's second return to consider in reflection to Acts 1:9–11 prophecy.

1) Jesus feet on the ground: Jesus ascended into heaven with his feet on the Mt. of Olives. Jesus's feet returning to the ground at the Mt. of Olives in Zechariah 14:4 is a reflection of this return, though is a different described event than the well-known 1 Thessalonians 4:17 meeting Jesus in the sky as a consequence of an earthly rapture. The previous verse 16, with the Lord returning from heaven to earth, seems a chronologically earlier event, supported earlier as at the midpoint. Therefore, verse 17 rapture must be considered a later event of Jesus continued presence.

2) Jesus's limited geographical group: A limited number of people saw Jesus when he ascended into heaven from the Mt. of Olives in Acts 1:9–12, as supported with 1 Corinthians 15:1–11. This is in contrast to the associated rapture with the consequential gathering in the sky, when all eyes will see Jesus (Rev. 1:7; cf. Matt. 24:30). This insight supports Jesus's parousia from heaven to earth occurring first and later His continued presence with the elect rapture.

3) Lightning flashes: Jesus's return will light up the sky from the west to the east (Matt. 24:27). This is reflective of the reverse direction in which Jesus left Jerusalem and made his way east to the Mt. of Olives (Acts 1:6–12).

4) Marvel at Jesus's coming: Previously 2 Thessalonians 1 and 2 was proposed at the midpoint when Jesus returns from heaven to earth. Verse 10 of the first chapter "to be marveled," is considered chronologically parallel to Matthew 24:17 with those on their housetops moments before they are commanded to flee from that same day abomination of desolation at the temple. Jesus's visual presence on or near the Mt. of Olives seems to be why those in Jerusalem are on their housetops marveling.

5) Thunder: It is unknown, for each of the seven proposed gatherings, whether God's voice will be heard in each person's native language or whether it will be heard as thunder as in John 12:28–29. Historically, God's presence is represented with thick clouds and a very loud trumpet blast as in Exodus 19:16.

6) Jesus's roaring as a Lion: The second return of Jesus will be as a roaring lion of Judah and not as a servant lamb as was his first coming. Satan is also described in 1 Peter 5:8 as a roaring lion, though he will later be captured by Jesus in Revelation 20:1–3.

GATHERINGS IN ZECH. 14:3 AND MATT. 24:17

The Greek word *episunagó* for gathering is not within Zechariah 14:3 and Matthew 24:17 where beyond prewrath proposes it to occur. Even so, we need to recognize that the opportunity for a gathering, of Jesus on the Mt. of Olives and those on their Jerusalem housetops, is reasonably derived. The two miles or less of unobstructed line of sight supports this. Since the Mt. of Olives has never been split in half and a wide valley formed, we know Zechariah 14 is a future prophecy. Acts 1:9–11 says Jesus will return in the same way, and he left from the Mt. of Olives in verse 12. There is enough circumstantial, scriptural evidence to support this claim of a gathering at the midpoint.

Consider that none of the premillennial views can reference a rapture (Greek *harpazó*) in the book of Revelation to support their rapture exegesis, though they all agree there will be a physical rapture before the millennium starts. They all use other Scriptures to support their chronological rapture exegesis as discussed in chapters 3, 5, and 6. There is a rapture in Revelation 12:5, though it is in reference to the historical ascension of Jesus. In the same way, the lack of an *episunagó* in the book of Revelation should not prevent us from chronologically placing it with the support of other Scriptures.

SEVEN GATHERINGS

The beyond prewrath proposes a total of seven eschatological gathering togethers which form a septet, which is eschatologically prevalent. A gathering always includes Jesus and the righteous. The righteous can include the following in any combination: the bride of Christ (church and Israel), and the sheep representing the subjects later being reigned over. Not all of the seven gatherings can be supported with the Greek word episunagó in Scripture, so it makes it a challenge to decide what is best.

Previously two gatherings were shown to exist in Scripture, the first is at the midpoint and a later as a consequence of the elect rapture where they meet Jesus in the sky. The following are the seven proposed opportunities for Jesus to have gatherings with the righteous.

1) The first is when Jesus returns the way he left to the Mt. of Olives at the midpoint. This is when those on their housetops (*not in the air as with the later gathering for a rapture*) see King Jesus (Isa. 33:17;

Zech. 14:4; Matt. 24:16–18; Acts 1:9–12; 2 Thess. 1:10, 2:1). This first gathering seems reflective of the Matthew 23:37 Jerusalem location.

> O Jerusalem, Jerusalem, the city that kills the prophets and stones those who are sent to it! How often would I have gathered your children together as a hen gathers her brood under her wings, and you were not willing! (Matt. 23:37)

2) It is only after those Jewish people have been in exile again that their next exodus can begin. This exodus seems to be reflective of the first exile in the book of Exodus. It begins when the worldwide great tribulation ends with the sixth opened seal (Matt. 24:29; Rev. 6:12). Then the Jewish people in exile would be gathered to make their way to Mt. Sinai with God possibly leading them with a cloud. There is agreement with the author Travis Snow that it seems those in exile would retrace their first exodus from the book of Exodus to Mt. Sinai.[1] Mt. Sinai is located in Arabia identified by Galatians 4:25. The presence of God could remain as a cloud on the mountain top until he leaves for the start of the sixth blown trumpet in Revelation 14:14. Mt. Sinai was where the Jewish people were betrothed to God in Exodus 19–20. This could represent more a manifestation of God than a gathering. This was also the location when the glory of God appeared to them when dedicating the tabernacle, and ordination of Moses, Aaran, and his sons in Leviticus 9:23.

3) The third gathering will be in the sky as a consequence of the elect rapture (Matt. 24:30–31; Rev. 1:7, 7:9–17, 8:5). It excludes the Jewish people from the Revelation 1:7 perspective since they are not in the sky with Jesus with the raptured elect though are mourning. The second reason is that the Jewish people are decreed to live through the last prophetic week (Dan. 9:24–25). They have so far only lived through the first 69 prophetic weeks. Daniel's prophetic clock restarts when the prince (little horn) makes the treaty-covenant strong as evident with a duration of seven years (Dan. 9:27).

4) There are two possible interpretations of when this fourth gathering could occur, which are during the sixth blown trumpet.

---

1   Travis M. Snow, *The Passover King: Exploring the Prophetic Connection between Passover, the End Times, and the Return of Jesus*, Dallas, Voice of Messiah, Inc., Dallas, Texas, © 2020.

a. The first and most likely interpretation is when the Lord pours out his spirit on Israel in Joel 2:28–29, which is before the great and awesome day of the Lord. Just prior to this gathering the bridegroom would leave his room in verses 15–16.

b. The second, though least likely interpretation, is when they gather to clear the blood from Jerusalem in Revelation 14:20. This verse represents after the Jehoshaphat battle when Jesus was alone in the battle (Isa. 63:3; Rev. 14:18–19). The day of this Jehoshaphat battle could include when warrior Jesus makes his way from Sinai to Edom (Deut. 33:1–2; Judg. 5:4–5; Ps. 63:1, 17; Isa. 63:1–6) or it could occur just prior. Since the Jewish people are not in the battle, it seems they trailed Jesus.

5) The fifth gathering is raptured Israel at the end of the seventieth week of Daniel (Rev. 11:19), when the bride of Christ (church and Israel) and the bridegroom Jesus attend the béma together in Revelation 11:18. Israel seems raptured laterally to Jerusalem and not to meet Jesus in the sky, as with the elect. This is posited since the second rejoicing in heaven is not until eight chapters after Israel is raptured (Rev. 11:19 versus 19:1–5) and second the béma is proposed to be in Jerusalem.

6) The sixth gathering is when the sheep are separated and gathered from the sheep and goat judgment (Matt. 25:31–46; Rev. 16:18) to attend the wedding supper as guests. This is derived with the support of Matthew 22:1–14. Scripture has the guests invited to the wedding feast, though not explicitly to the wedding.

7) The seventh gathering is when Jesus leads the armies of heaven to make war against the wicked in the Armageddon battle (Rev. 19:11–21, 20:1–3; cf. 16:16).

Blow the trumpet in Zion;
> consecrate a fast;
call a solemn assembly;
> gather the people.
Consecrate the congregation;
> assemble the elders;
gather the children,
> even nursing infants.
Let the bridegroom leave his room,
> and the bride her chamber.
(Joel 2:15–16)

FIGURE 3: SEVEN GATHERINGS

Gathering sequence	When	Location	Who
First	Midpoint	Mt. of Olives, Jerusalem	Those on their housetops
Second	Sixth seal to fifth trumpet	Exodus to Mt. Sinai	Jewish people
Third	End of seventh seal	Worldwide	All will see Jesus. Church raptured to sky
Fourth	Sixth trumpet	Worldwide	Israel receives the Lord's spirit
Fifth	Day 1,260	Jerusalem	Béma: Church and Israel
Sixth	Seventh bowl	Wedding supper at Jerusalem	Church, Israel, and sheep
Seventh	Seventh bowl	Armies at Armageddon in Israel	Church and Israel

THREE PAIRS: GATHERINGS AND DAYS OF THE LORD

Beyond prewrath proposes at least two eschatological pairs of gatherings and same day "day of the Lord." Most scholars have only one chronological pair. That is, they incorrectly equate 2 Thessalonians 2:1–4 pair with the

Lot and Noah prophecy pair of Luke 17:22–37. Beyond prewrath has these as two separate chronological pairs represented as the first two pairs below.

1) The first pair is with 2 Thessalonians 2:1–4, which other Scriptures within figures 1 and 2 pinpointed at the midpoint. The gathering is for those on their Jerusalem housetops (Matt. 24:17) and Jesus coming to the Mt. of Olives (Zech. 14:4; Matt. 24:27; Acts 1:9–12). The day of the Lord is representative of Zechariah 14:1.

2) The second pair is in the seventh opened seal where the church gathers with Jesus in the sky (Matt. 24:30–31) as a consequence of the elect rapture (Rev. 8:5) followed by the same day "day of the Lord" in the first blown trumpet (Rev. 8:7). This is reflective of Noah's righteous family of eight gathered together with the Lord closing the door of the ark and the same day when the wicked were destroyed with the flood (Gen. 7:11–21).

3) There appears to be a third chronological pair within the seventh poured bowl where the righteous, clothed in white linen, are gathered with Jesus for the Armageddon battle against the wicked that same day "day of the Lord" as described in Revelation 19:11 to 20:3.[2]

RESURRECTION WITH JESUS COMING

The Second Coming of Jesus—from heaven to earth—is described in Scripture as occurring "with all His saints" (1 Thess. 3:13), indicating a concurrent event. His coming is proposed to take place at the midpoint (fifth seal of the great tribulation), which appears to align with a resurrection of dead (Dan. 12:2; 1 Cor. 15:52). According to the beyond prewrath dispensational understanding, the rapture of the elect (Matt. 24:30–31; 1

---

2   Some may claim, from the chapter break, that Revelation 20:1–3 chronologically belongs in the millennium with the verses 4–5. Consider if Satan was captured at the start of the millennium when Jesus and those with him started their earthly reign for a thousand years. Then after Satan's release of a thousand years, it would give no time for him to mount an attack against Jerusalem near its end in verses 7–10. Basically, Revelation 20:1–3 should have been placed at the end of Revelation 19 as verses 22–24, as a consequence of the Armageddon battle when the beast, the false prophet, and the rest were also captured in 19:20–21.

Thess. 4:17–18; Rev. 8:5) is associated with the seventh seal, suggesting a resurrection (John 5:28–29) occurs earlier in the prophetic timeline.

Nowhere in Scripture is it explicitly stated that the resurrection and the elect rapture happen on the same day, as some premillennial proponents claim. Rather, 1 Thessalonians 4:13–18 simply requires that the resurrection precedes the catching up of the living.

> For the Lord himself will descend from heaven with a cry of command, with the voice of an archangel, and with the sound of the trumpet of God. And the dead in Christ will rise first. (1 Thess. 4:16)

THE LAST TRUMPET

The Beyond Prewrath view interprets the "last trumpet" in 1 Corinthians 15:52 (cf. 1 Thess. 4:13–17), which signals the resurrection of the dead, as corresponding to the third and final angelic proclamation in Revelation 14:9–11. This is seen as occurring at the midpoint of the 70th week and marking the return of Jesus, as supported in chapter 1. In the Old Testament, proclamations were often associated with trumpet blasts (e.g., Num. 10:2–3; Joel 2:1).

The first angel's message in Revelation 14:6–7, announcing the "eternal gospel," is viewed as chronologically parallel to Matthew 24:14, where "the gospel of the kingdom will be proclaimed," just before the abomination of desolation described in verse 15 (cf. Dan. 9:27). Both the pretribulation and prewrath positions lack a scriptural basis for interpreting the event with two or more trumpets, which is necessary to identify a definitive "last trumpet."

CONCLUSION

The return of Jesus must be reflective of Acts 1:11, which says, "[He] will come in the same way as you saw him go into heaven." Verse 12 says that the apostles then "returned to Jerusalem from the mount called Olivet, which is near Jerusalem." Therefore, Jesus must return to the Mt. of Olives, which is on the ground and not reflective of a consequential rapture with meeting Jesus in the air (Rev. 1:7). Jesus returns with His resurrected saints at the last trumpet. Figures 1 and 2 supported Jesus's parousia from heaven to earth at the midpoint with a gathering and day of the Lord, reflective of 2 Thessalonians 2:1–4.

There is then strong support that Jesus's first gathering together (Greek *episynagōgēs*) is with those nearby on their Jerusalem housetops. Moments later the Jewish remnant will sense danger from the abomination of desolation and three world-wide angel proclamations, and then flee. Those who flee east through the wide valley just formed from the earthquake are granted by God relief from Satan's persecution for three and a half years.

The coming (Greek *parousia*) of both Jesus and Satan, from heaven to earth, will occur at the midpoint of the seventieth week of Daniel. The midpoint abomination of desolation (Dan. 9:27; Matt. 24:15) opens the fifth seal of the great tribulation and Jacob's trouble, which is an unparalleled time of persecution (Jer. 30:7). The Lord then responds on this day with a day of the Lord. The Scriptures in figure 2 provided support that the first and second chapters of 2 Thessalonians occur at the midpoint, but not for a rapture.

At least two chronological pairs of gatherings and a same day "day of the Lord" have been proposed and not the scholarly interpreted one. The first pair is for Jesus's coming (Matt. 24:27) from heaven to earth and the second pair is a continued presence for the church rapture (Matt. 24:30–31). The seventh reason of chapter 6 will later point out that these verses are separated by verse 29, which is identified as the sixth opened seal of Revelation 6:12–17. This identified sixth opened seal verse of Matthew 24:29 with darkness forces the understanding that Jesus coming in verse 27 is chronologically earlier in the fifth opened seal and the rapture of the elect is chronologically later in verses 30–31, identified in the seventh opened seal of Revelation 8:5 theophany. A third pair is proposed, and possibly a fourth, though they do not have the significance of the first two.

Jesus returns to Jerusalem, though not on the exact day of His return from heaven to the Mt. of Olives. He is proposed to arrive in Jerusalem later, likely in the sixth blown trumpet as proposed in *Jesus's Return based on the Feasts of the Lord.*

Chapter 2

Seven Unique Days of the Lord

INTRODUCTION

The eschatological framework presents seven distinct days of the Lord. Regardless of one's premillennial perspective, this new interpretation may prove surprising. Building upon the previous chapter's assertion that the day of the Lord referenced in 2 Thessalonians 2:1–3 occurs chronologically at the midpoint of the seventieth week, it follows that the elect's rapture takes place after the great tribulation, as evidenced by Revelation 7:9–17. This uniquely different gathering (in the sky versus on the ground) and its associated day of the Lord, as with Lot and Noah, suggests the existence of at least two eschatological days of the Lord.

DAY OF THE LORD VERSUS WRATH OF GOD

An eschatological day of the Lord represents a specific manifestation of God's wrath against the wicked. This day, characterized by the presence of Jesus Christ and its inherently negative aspect, can range from a mild form—illustrated by individuals seeking refuge in the rocks during the wrath of the Lamb in the sixth seal—to more severe manifestations, such as the three battles of Jesus.[1]

The wrath of God, on the other hand, constitutes a broader category encompassing various forms of punishment inflicted upon the wicked, with or without the direct presence of Jesus. Fundamentally, the day of the Lord should be viewed as a subset of divine wrath. In some instances, the wrath of God comprises only angels, as seen in the first to fourth blown trumpets. The fifth trumpet introduces an attacking force of apocalyptic locusts emerging from the bottomless pit. Each of the seven blown trumpets and seven poured bowls constitutes an instance of the wrath of God (Rev. 15:1). Additionally, there are manifestations of divine wrath at the midpoint and within the sixth seal.

---

1   Robert Van Kampen in *The Sign of Christ's Coming and the End of the Age* introduced the names of the first two battles: Jerusalem and Jehoshaphat. The third battle Armageddon is well-known.

TWO TYPES OF DAYS OF THE LORD

Two distinct types of days of the Lord are proposed based on their chronological placement relative to the midpoint. This book directs its focus towards the eschatological days of the Lord spanning from the midpoint until fifteen months after the beast is captured, totaling seven in number. It is notable that the significance of this midpoint, marked by the crucial chronological division delineated by the three worldwide angel proclamations, often goes unrecognized by most scholars.

FIRST TYPE DAY OF THE LORD (BEFORE MIDPOINT)

A day of the Lord occurring prior to the midpoint can be interpreted as targeting either the wicked or the righteous. An illustration of such a day of the Lord is found in Zephaniah 1:7–9, depicting punishment directed toward certain Jewish officials. Considering the covenantal relationship between the Jewish people and God, established in Exodus 19:7–8, any punishment inflicted upon them can aptly be understood as chastisement against his betrothed Jewish bride. This chastisement serves as a corrective measure, motivated by God's love and the desire to turn away from sinful behavior. Scripture reveals instances where God relents from His wrath upon witnessing genuine repentance. The inhabitants of Nineveh provide a notable example as they repented of their sins through fasting and humble supplication before God, though they were not Jewish.

Those who persist in their refusal to repent endure divine chastisement. However, it is important to note that even amidst chastisement, there remains an opportunity for individuals to repent of their sins and reconcile with God. This window of opportunity closes at the midpoint with the third angel proclamation, as discussed further in the subsequent exploration of a different type of day of the Lord.

SECOND TYPE DAY OF THE LORD (MIDPOINT PLUS)

A second type of day of the Lord begins at about the midpoint. This is when the three angelic proclamations are made worldwide. Those who disregard the instructions outlined in the third angel's proclamation, as described in Revelation 14:9–11, face the dire consequences of eternal damnation in hell. The decision to disobey this proclamation becomes irrevocable while still alive on earth, as indicated in 2 Thessalonians 2:11 where a strong delusion is said to befall those who reject the truth. In this eschatological context, the Holy Spirit does not relent, meaning that individuals who receive the mark of the beast and worship their image will be unable to repent while still living on earth.

DAY OF CHRIST VERSUS THE DAY OF THE LORD

A clear distinction must be drawn between the eschatological day of the Lord and the day of Christ. The day of the Lord is invariably linked with judgment, serving as a time of reckoning for humanity. In contrast, the day of Christ is synonymous with eternal reward and blessing, manifesting in the resurrection of the dead and the rapture of the living. Interestingly, my interpretation aligns with that of the Scofield Study Bible's pretribulation commentary on 1 Corinthians 1:8: "Who will sustain you to the end, guiltless in the day of the Lord Jesus Christ."

> The expression "the day of our Lord Jesus Christ," identified with His coming (v. 7), is the period of blessing for the Church beginning with the rapture. This coming day is referred to as "the day of the Lord Jesus" (1 Cor. 5:5; 2 Cor. 1:4), "the day of Christ Jesus" (Phil. 1:6), and "the day of Christ" (Phil. 1:10; 2:16). In all six references in the N.T., this "day" relates to the reward and blessing of the Church at the rapture in contrast with the expression "the day of the LORD" (compare Isa. 2:12; Joel 1:15, note; Rev. 19:19, note), which is related to judgment on unbelieving Jews and Gentiles, and blessing on millennial saints (Zeph. 3:8–20).[2]

THREE DAYS OF CHRIST (RAPTURES)

The references to the day of Christ (Phil. 1:10; 2:16), the day of Jesus Christ (Phil. 1:6), and the day of our Lord Jesus Christ (2 Cor. 1:14) all signify the righteous receiving their eternal salvation through a rapture or resurrection event. It is widely understood as a day of Christ. Three distinct chronological types of rapture groups are proposed.

---

2   Scofield Reference Bible commentary on 1 Corinthians 1:8, NASB, Oxford University Press, Inc., © 1967, 1614.

The first two groups consist of the Church and Israel, selected based on their faith. The third group is inferred to be the sheep, represented as the third great theophany in Revelation 16:18, although their selection criteria, as outlined in Matthew 25:31–46, differ from those of the first two groups. Notably, the selection process for this group is based on works rather than faith (vv. 35–36).

MIDPOINT PAROUSIA OF JESUS AND SATAN

Parousia, as defined in *Strong's Concordance*, is a Greek noun meaning "a presence" or "a coming," though its usage is not exclusively limited to the return of Christ. The term is described as a "technical term with reference to the visit of a king or some other official," often denoting a royal visitation.[3] Nowhere in this definition is its application restricted solely to blessings. Thus, parousia could also be interpreted in a negative context, as evidenced by its association with Satan in 2 Thessalonians 2:9 and his expulsion from heaven in Revelation 12:7–12.

The parousia of both Christ and Satan, from heaven to earth, occurs at the midpoint. Christ's parousia is depicted with his feet landing on the Mt. of Olives, as indicated in Zechariah 14:3–4. Conversely, Satan's parousia coincides with his expulsion from heaven and subsequent spiritual indwelling into the man of lawlessness, marking the emergence of the Antichrist, who instigates the abomination of desolation in the Jewish temple. The proximity of these two earthly arrival locations, separated by a distance of less than a mile, suggests the possibility of Jesus and the Antichrist encountering each other initially at the midpoint.

SEVEN DAYS OF THE LORD

The beyond prewrath perspective posits the existence of seven eschatological days of the Lord, contrasting with the traditional premillennial viewpoint, which typically acknowledges only one.

---

3   James Strong, *Strong's Exhaustive Concordance of the Bible*, Bible Hub, s.v. "3952 parousia," accessed September 8, 2023, https://biblehub.com/greek/3952.htm.

FIRST DAY OF THE LORD – JERUSALEM BATTLE

The initial day of the Lord, as recorded in Zechariah 14:1, is referred to as the Jerusalem battle due to the gathering of nations for conflict in that location (v. 2). This marks the onset of Jesus's first of three battles. This also begins a time of distress for Jacob (Israel) described in Jeremiah 30:7, Daniel 12:1, and in general (Matt. 24:21) as a persecution unparalleled in history,[4] this day of the Lord is specifically directed against the wicked within and around Jerusalem. Matthew 24:15–16 and Daniel 9:27 collectively document its commencement at the midpoint.

In Figures 1 and 2, the scriptural parallels substantiate Jesus's return at the Mt. of Olives at the midpoint, coinciding with the gathering mentioned in 2 Thessalonians 2:1 and a day of the Lord (vv. 1–2). This day of the Lord appears to be a consequence of Gog's initial assault on Israel with the midpoint abomination of desolation, prompting the remnant of Israel to flee (Zech. 14:5; Matt. 24:17). Despite Gog's, and his ten kings, significant efforts (Ezek. 38:1–16; Zech. 13:7–8), they do not achieve complete success as the Lord responds on the same day with a targeted day of the Lord against the wicked, as outlined in Ezekiel 38:17–23 and the initial verses of Zechariah 14. This lack of absolute success mirrors Gog's subsequent second and third attack in Ezekiel 39.[5]

It is noteworthy that God grants the prince (man) and Satan (spirit) the authority to wage war against the saints and prevail over them in Daniel 7:25 and Revelation 12:7–17, respectively. Together they represent the plural Antichrist, who comes into existence when Satan is thrown out of heaven. This authorization is conferred despite Jesus being the only one worthy to break the seven seals and unveil the scroll contents (Rev. 5). Thus, God does not compel Satan to wage war against the saints; it is inherent to his nature to kill and destroy.

---

4 Joel 2:2 cannot be included in this list since it is in reference to a great and powerful people, which is a different context than unparalleled persecution. This Scripture is applicable to the fifth blown trumpet and not the midpoint with the opening of the fifth seal, which starts the great tribulation.

5 See chapter 7.

SECOND DAY OF THE LORD – WRATH OF THE LAMB

The second day of the Lord is perceived as relatively mild in its impact upon the wicked, as evidenced by the absence of explicit death targeted against them in the sixth seal of Revelation 6:12–17. Instead, they experience a sense of wanting death (sixth seal), though later (seventh seal) that of humility, as depicted in Isaiah 2:12, 18–19.[6]

THIRD DAY OF THE LORD – FIRST BLOWN TRUMPET

The third day of the Lord coincides with the event of the church rapture. This synchronicity mirrors Jesus's prophecy in the Olivet Discourse, likening the situation to that of Noah and Lot where the righteous were physically separated on the same day preceding the onset of the day of the Lord against the wicked. In the beyond prewrath perspective, this day of the Lord unfolds in Revelation 8:7 after the elect rapture earlier described in Revelation 8:5 theophany. Essentially, verses 5, 6, and 7 transpire on the same Jewish day.

WRATH OF GOD – FIFTH BLOWN TRUMPET

The fifth blown trumpet is not considered a day of the Lord since Jesus is not explicitly present, though just a wrath of God. This analysis will later support the discussion of the Garden of Eden in Chapter 7. It is described as a great and magnificent day in Joel 2:11, it spans a duration of five months characterized by apocalyptic horror. This period is so dire that individuals will actively seek death but will be unable to find it. The locusts unleashed in this event originate from the furnace of the bottomless pit, identified as Hades (Joel 2:1–11; Rev. 9:1–11). Refer to figure 4 below for parallel supporting Scriptures.

---

6   See chapter 6, Prewrath Chronology Problems: First Reason – Wrath of the Lamb.

FIGURE 4: WRATH OF GOD – LOCUST TORMENT

Joel 2	Amos 5/ Zechariah 14	Revelation 8, 9
Trumpet blown (v. 1)		Fifth angel's trumpet blown (9:1)
Day of darkness (v. 2)	Darkness (Amos 5: 18, 20)	The sun darkened (9:2)
Fire before and after (v. 3)		Fire before and after (8:10; 9:18)
Garden of Eden before (v. 3)	Flesh will rot (Zech. 14:12). Three years later garden of Eden.	
Appearance of horses (v. 4)		Locusts appear like horses (9:7)
Greatness of the day of the Lord (v. 11)	Day of the Lord like a man fleeing a lion to meet a bear or being bitten by a snake (Amos 5:18–19)	Allowed to torment but not kill (9:5)

FIRST ROW: FIFTH TRUMPET

The events depicted collectively contribute to the narrative of the fifth blown trumpet.

SECOND ROW: DARKNESS

One of the infrequent, though significant themes in Scripture is the imagery of darkness. Throughout the seventieth week of Daniel and the thirty days of the poured bowls, darkness is mentioned for at least five events. Amidst a total of twenty-one chronological events (comprising seven opened seals, seven blown trumpets, and seven poured bowls). These instances include part of Day 1 in the fifth seal, the sixth seal, the fifth trumpet, part of the sixth trumpet, and the fifth bowl.[7] This scarcity of darkness-themed events helps to pinpoint the chronological placement of eschatological Scripture.

---

7   See pages 53–54 of *Beyond Prewrath End-Time Prophecy.*

THIRD ROW: FIRE BEFORE AND AFTER

Another recurring theme among these Scriptures is the imagery of fire: "fire devours before them, and behind them a flame burns" (Joel 2:3a). The fire before is evident when the third trumpet sounds: "The third angel blew his trumpet, and a great star fell from heaven, blazing like a torch" (Rev. 8:10a). The fire after is depicted when the sixth blown trumpet sounds: "By these three plagues a third of mankind was killed, by the fire" (Rev. 9:18a). These Scriptures, taken together, contribute to identifying the third eschatological day of the Lord as occurring either at the fourth or fifth blown trumpet.

FOURTH ROW: GARDEN OF EDEN

The concept of a garden of Eden-like landscape in eschatological terms, as mentioned in Joel 2:3b, presents a unique challenge considering the current state of Israel's agricultural landscape. The interpretation proposed suggests that the soil at the battlefield location of the Jerusalem battle at the midpoint becomes productive due to the presence of blood and pulverized human bones, which enrich the soil over the course of approximately three years[8] leading up to the fifth blown trumpet. Furthermore, the living water flowing (Zech. 14:8) at the midpoint contributes to soil fertility. Additionally, it is worth noting that while the early trumpet judgments bring destruction to portions of the earth, they do not entail complete devastation.

Regarding the references to fire, the occurrence of fire before is observed in the second blown trumpet (Rev. 8:8–9) while the first instance of fire after is depicted in part of the sixth blown trumpet (Rev. 9:13–19). Notably, the third blown trumpet involves a blazing fallen star that strikes the water but does not affect the terrain, suggesting that it would not initiate fires that would impact the garden of Eden like terrain until later. Ezekiel 36:35 describes the garden of Eden during the millennium.

---

8   Second half of seventieth week is three and a half years. Removing the fifth trumpet duration of five months (Rev. 9:5) leaves about three years to bleach into soil. See chapter 11 of *Jesus's Return based on the Feasts of the Lord.*

Fire devours before them,
   and behind them a flame burns.
The land is like the garden of Eden before them,
   but behind them a desolate wilderness,
   and nothing escapes them.
(Joel 2:3)

FIFTH ROW: HORSES

A recurring theme in Joel 2:4 is the appearance of horses, which, when considered alongside other thematic elements, aids in pinpointing its association with the fourth day of the Lord. This aligns with the imagery in Revelation 9:7 where the locusts are described as resembling horses.

SIXTH ROW: PEOPLE SEEK DEATH

The depiction of people seeking death due to torment, as described in Revelation 9:6, is a chilling aspect of the apocalyptic horror associated with the locusts emerging from the bottomless pit. This portrayal mirrors the torment inflicted by the locusts, originating from the great furnace of the bottomless pit, and essentially brings a glimpse of hell to earth for a duration of five months.

BRIDEGROOM LEAVES HIS CHAMBER

The imagery of the bridegroom Jesus leaving his room in Joel 2:16 precedes the description of the great and awesome day of the Lord (commonly associated with the Jehoshaphat battle) mentioned in Joel 2:30–32, coinciding with the blowing of the sixth trumpet. Chapter 11 of *Jesus's Return based on the Feasts of the Lord* provides numerous chronological details pertaining to the events surrounding the sixth and seventh blown trumpets.

Considering that the coming of Jesus, from heaven to earth, commenced earlier at the midpoint, it is not possible that Jesus is later depicted as leaving his heavenly abode since there is only one second coming, from heaven to earth. Rather, the room referenced here likely pertains to a chamber within the yet-to-be-built third temple in Jerusalem. Notably, while the outer court of the temple is mentioned as being given over to the nations (Rev. 11:2), there is no explicit reference to the inner court.

FOURTH DAY OF THE LORD – JEHOSHAPHAT BATTLE

The fourth day of the Lord transpires within the sounding of the sixth trumpet. One of the events occurring then is the Jehoshaphat battle, as described in Joel 3:2. This battle marks the second of three battles involving Jesus. The great and awesome day of the Lord depicted in Joel 2:28–32 and Malachi 4:1–5 is synonymous with the Jehoshaphat battle, with those being spiritually saved preceding this pivotal event. Parallel Scriptures detailing events surrounding the Jehoshaphat battle are provided in the figure below.

FIGURE 5: FOURTH DAY OF THE LORD – JEHOSHAPHAT

Isaiah and Joel	Revelation 9	Revelation 11 and 14	Malachi 4
Trumpet blown; Bridegroom leaves his room (Joel 2:15)	Blown trumpet 6 (v. 13)	Son of man on a cloud (14:14)	
The Valley of Jehoshaphat (Joel 3:2)		Prior to start of blown trumpet 7 (11:15)	
	Four angels (v. 14)	Four angels (14:14–15; 17–18)	
Sickle winepress overflowing because evil is great (Joel 3:13)		Sharp sickle; winepress of the wrath of God (14:17, 19)	
Sun darkened before day of the Lord (Joel 2:31)		No reference to clouds (darkness) (14:19)	
Day of the Lord (Joel 3:14)		Wrath of God (14:19)	"Great and awesome day" (v.5)

FIGURE 5 (*continued*)

Isaiah and Joel	Revelation 9	Revelation 11 and 14	Malachi 4
Blood and fire; year of recompense and soil into sulfur (Isa. 34:8–9; Joel 2:30)	Fire, smoke, and sulfur (vv. 17–18)	Authority of third angel over fire (14:18)	Evildoers set ablaze (v. 1)
	One-third of mankind killed (v. 18)	Blood up to a horse's bridle (14:20)	Wicked tread down (v. 3)
Gathering (Joel 2:16)	Horsemen (vv. 16–17)	Horse bridle (indicates horsemen) (14:20)	

SIXTH POURED BOWL – ARMAGEDDON LOGISTICS

Before the Armageddon battle ensues, the sixth poured bowl depicts the logistical movement of the kings from the east as they traverse in a westward direction across the dried Euphrates River bed to convene for battle at a location known as Armageddon (Rev. 16:16). The subsequent verse initiates the seventh poured bowl, which sets the stage for the forthcoming battle. The details of this battle and its aftermath are further elaborated upon in Revelation 19:11 to 20:3.

MARRIAGE OF THE LAMB – REVELATION 19:6–8

The marriage of the Lamb is an event exclusively for the bride of Christ, comprising both the Church and Israel. Its occurrence appears to coincide with the pouring of the seventh bowl. The chronology of this event is indicated in Revelation 19:6, which describes "the voice of a great multitude like the roar of many waters and like the sound of mighty peals of thunder."

During this momentous occasion, the bride of Christ is adorned in fine linen, bright and pure, symbolizing her righteousness and purity (Rev. 19:8).

FIFTH DAY OF THE LORD – SHEEP AND GOATS

Following the marriage of the Lamb, Revelation 19:9–10 portrays the wedding feast of the Lamb, celebrating the union of Jesus, the bridegroom, with the bride of Christ. Those seeking entry to the feast are the sheep and goats from the third great dispensational theophany outlined in Revelation 16:18. The separation of the sheep and goats for entry is determined by their actions as described in Matthew 25:31–46, specifically regarding their treatment of Jesus's brothers, which refers to followers of Jesus (Matt. 12:46–50).

The goats, having shown none of the acts of kindness outlined in Matthew 25:42–43, are considered the wicked and are consequently denied entry to the wedding feast represented as a day of the Lord. Conversely, the sheep, who exhibited kindness to Jesus's brothers, are in verse 34 "blessed by my Father" and deemed worthy to inherit the millennial kingdom, represented as a day of Christ. These sheep are invited to partake in the wedding feast as guests, symbolized by their possession of wedding garments (Matt. 22:11). Conversely, the goats are refused entry due to their lack of wedding garments (Matt. 22:12–13). The wedding garments of the sheep appear to represent a spiritual covering indicative of their actions and their alignment with the will of God.

SIXTH DAY OF THE LORD – ARMAGEDDON

Following the completion of the wedding supper, Jesus, accompanied by the bride, engages in the Armageddon battle, which unfolds with the pouring out of the seventh bowl (Rev. 19:11–21; cf. Rev. 16:12–16). This climactic conflict occurs on the "great day of God the Almighty" (Rev. 16:14b), recognized as the seventh day of the Lord.

The saints who participated in the marriage of the Lamb are depicted as clothed in "fine linen, bright and pure" (Rev. 19:8), suggesting their involvement in the Armageddon battle. This is supported by Revelation 19:14, which portrays the armies of heaven adorned in similar attire, following Jesus into battle. However, there is no indication that the sheep will partake in this battle as there is no mention of them wearing fine linen.

During the battle, both the beast (the man of lawlessness) and the false prophet will be captured and cast into the lake of fire (Rev. 19:19–20). Satan, however, will be captured but kept alive for a thousand years before being temporarily released for a little while prior to the conclusion of Jesus's earthly millennial reign (Rev. 20:1–3).

SHEEP ARE REIGNED OVER IN THE MILLENNIUM

In the onset of the millennium on earth, the sheep, considered the works-based "blessed by my Father" subjects, will be governed by Jesus from the Jerusalem throne for a duration of a thousand years. There are two lower judicial support systems. The first are the apostles who judge over the twelve tribes in Luke 22:28–30. The second who judge over those remaining on earth, comprised of those who were martyred for their testimony of Jesus will assist in administering justice during this period (Rev. 20:4–5).

Matthew 25:46 says that the righteous, represented by the sheep, will attain eternal life. However, this raises the question of why the sheep, whose earthly separation was based on works rather than faith (Matt. 25:35–36), would be given eternal spiritual life. One plausible explanation is that upon their rapture and subsequent participation in the wedding supper, upon seeing the bridegroom Jesus, they immediately profess Jesus as their Lord and Savior. Consequently, they become the individuals who share their faith to their descendants born during the millennium. These sheep entering the millennium are expected to enjoy longevity akin to the patriarchs before the flood.

> And these will go away into eternal punishment (goats), but the righteous (sheep) into eternal life. (Matt. 25:46)

SEVENTH DAY OF THE LORD – BEASTS SURVIVE

There is likely a seventh Day of the Lord to complete a septet. This could be represented by the death of some or all of the ten beasts fifteen months after the millennium begins (Dan. 7:11–12). However, it may be more closely associated with an event during the seven blown trumpets or the seven poured bowls.

CONCLUSION

Beyond prewrath challenges the prevailing premillennial perspective by proposing the existence of seven distinct eschatological days of the Lord, contrary to the notion of just one. This viewpoint asserts that the eschatological wrath of God, serving as judgment against the wicked, can be further categorized into a day of the Lord when God's presence is manifest. For instance, during the fifth blown trumpet, where only locusts from the bottomless pit and angels are present, Jesus is notably absent, indicating a generic wrath of God.

The midpoint of the seventieth week marks a crucial juncture with two distinct parousias or comings. Jesus's and Satan's parousia, from heaven to earth, commences with a gathering in 2 Thessalonians 2:1 and Matthew 24:17, followed that day by a day of the Lord in Zechariah 14:1.

FIGURE 6: DAYS OF THE LORD AND OF CHRIST

Event	Description	When	Judgment / Blessing
First day of the Lord	Jerusalem Battle	Day 1	Judgment
Second day of the Lord	Wrath of the Lamb	Opened sixth and seventh seals	Judgment (wicked brought low)
First day of Christ	First theophany: Resurrection and rapture	Last day of opened seal 7	Blessing (Rapture)
Third day of the Lord	Wrath of God	Blown trumpet 1	Judgment
Fourth day of the Lord	Jehoshaphat Battle	Blown trumpet 6	Judgment
Second day of the Christ	Second theophany	Blown trumpet 7	Blessing (Rapture)
Day of Christ and Lord	Third theophany: Sheep and goats	Poured bowl 7	Blessing (Rapture) and Judgment
Great Day of God Almighty	Armageddon Battle	Poured bowl 7	Judgment
Day of the Lord	Some beasts survive	15 months after beast killed	Judgment

Chapter 3

Pretribulation Problems

PURPOSE

The purpose of this discussion is to explore different premillennial rapture views, highlighting their areas of agreement. Following this, we will delve into several exegesis problems associated with pretribulation.

FIVE DIFFERENT RAPTURE TIMING VIEWS

The figure below utilizes the concept of the wrath of God rather than the day of the Lord to distinguish between each view. Both prewrath and beyond prewrath depict the rapture of the church as chronologically close, represented by the same upward arrow indicating a rapture. However, for simplicity, what the figure doesn't show is that beyond prewrath includes two later raptures. Also, it does not illustrate the beyond prewrath wrath of God at the midpoint, in the sixth opened seal, trumpet judgments, bowl judgments, and fifteen months after the beast is killed.

FIGURE 7: FIVE RAPTURE POSITIONS

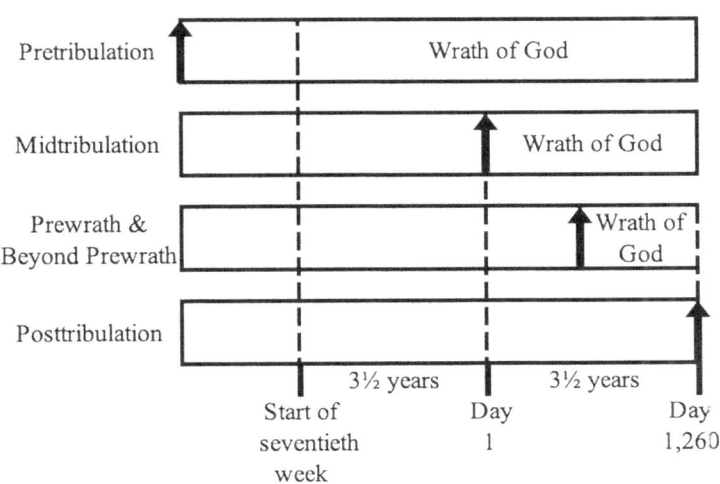

PREMILLENNIAL AGREEMENTS

The following provides a list of the premillennial agreements among the five different rapture positions.

FIRST – RIGHTEOUS NOT APPOINTED GOD'S WRATH

The first agreement is that all premillennial rapture views concur that the righteous are not destined for the wrath of God, as 1 Thessalonians 5:9 says, "For God has not destined us for wrath, but to obtain salvation through our Lord Jesus Christ." However, from the beyond prewrath view, it is essential to note that this does not preclude the possibility of God's wrath being directed against the wicked while the righteous remain on earth. A pertinent example is found in the story of Lot and his family, who escaped the wrath of God on the same day it befell Sodom, yet they still resided on earth.

SECOND – RAPTURE IS A PHYSICAL EVENT

The second agreement is that all premillennial rapture views also concur that the rapture will be a physical event rather than purely spiritual. The physical nature of the rapture is described in passages such as 1 Thessalonians 4:13–18 and 1 Corinthians 15:50–54. However, it is worth noting that these passages do not provide a chronological context for the rapture relative to the events of the seventieth week of Daniel, which includes the seven opened seals and seven blown trumpets.

THIRD – JESUS REIGNS DURING MILLENNIUM

All premillennial views agree that Jesus's physical reign on earth is for a thousand years sometime after the seventieth week (Rev. 20:4–5; cf. Isa. 65:18–25; Matt. 25:31–40). It is noted, though not uniformly recognized, there are lower judicial courts (Luke 22:28–30; Rev. 20:4–5).

FOURTH – 70 WEEKS ARE DECREED

All will agree that 69 weeks have been fulfilled and that one seventieth week is prophetically remaining.

PRETRIBULATION PROBLEMS

The following are seven pretribulation problems. There are other scholarly books identifying pretribulation problems.[1]

FIRST – JESUS'S PAROUSIA THEN RAPTURE

Pretribulation doctrine is distinct among the premillennial views in asserting that the church rapture occurs before the coming of Jesus. However, it raises questions about how a gathering in the sky with Jesus and the righteous, as a consequence of a rapture, would not represent an occurrence of Jesus's coming at that moment. Some proponents attempt to address this objection by suggesting that the rapture is secretly done, although Revelation 1:7 indicates otherwise, stating that all eyes will see Jesus in the clouds.[2]

In contrast, beyond prewrath positions Jesus's coming, from heaven to earth, at the midpoint, as supported in Chapter 1. Consequently, it becomes untenable for the pretribulation rapture to occur before this midpoint.

> Then will appear in heaven the sign of the Son of Man, and then all the tribes of the earth will mourn, and *they will see the Son of Man coming on the clouds of heaven with power and great glory.* (Matt. 24:30, emphasis added)

> Behold, he is coming with the clouds, and *every eye will see him, even those who pierced him,* and all tribes of the earth will wail on account of him. Even so. Amen. (Rev. 1:7, emphasis added)

SECOND – NO REVELATION 4 REJOICING IN HEAVEN

Many pretribulation proponents have their physical rapture in Revelation 4:1 when the apostle John's spirit arrives in heaven. The problem is that this chapter has no multitude rejoicing as with the later Revelation 7:9–17, which is within the seventieth week of Daniel. The pretribulation rapture call those who come to Jesus in faith during the seventieth week as the

---

1   Alan E. Kurschner, *Pretrib Examining the Foundations of Pretribulation Rapture Theology,* Eschatos Publishing, © 2022 and Nelson Walters, *Rapture: Case Closed?,* Ready for Jesus Publications, © 2017.

2   *ESV Study Bible,* Crossway, Wheaton, Illinois, www.crossway.org, © 2008, 2697.

"tribulation saints." The absence of rejoicing and a multitude in Revelation 4 suggests that there is no rapture depicted in that chapter, leading to questions regarding the timing and nature of the pretribulation rapture. Any chronological rapture exegesis based on silence should be considered weak, if it holds any merit at all.

THIRD – JESUS DID NOT ASCEND ON A HORSE

Pretribulation and posttribulation proponents believe that Jesus will return, from heaven to earth, for the Armageddon battle on a white horse (Rev. 19:11). According to the beyond prewrath premise set in Chapter 1 with Acts 1:9–11, Jesus "will come in the same way as you saw him go into heaven." Since Jesus did not ascend into heaven on a horse, his return from heaven to earth must exclude him riding a horse. However, chronologically later, during the pouring of the seventh bowl, Jesus's continued presence is expected to be marked by his appearance on a white horse at the Armageddon battle.

FOURTH – CHURCH IN REVELATION 4 TILL 19?

Occasionally, the pretribulation perspective asserts that the church is not mentioned in the book of Revelation from 4:1 until chapter 19 because the Greek word *kyriakos* for "church" is absent. Therefore, they argue, the church must have been physically raptured when the spirit of the apostle John was taken to heaven in Revelation 4:1.

The majority of instances where *kyriakos* is used refer to the seven sister churches of Revelation 2–3, which is expected given the context. Nonetheless, a careful examination reveals that there are indeed many references to the church from Revelation 4:1 to chapter 19, albeit without the exact use of the word *kyriakos*. This suggests that the church is indeed present during at least a portion of the seventieth week of Daniel.

1) Revelation 6:9–11 has "those who had been slain for the word of God and for the witness they had borne."

2) Figure 8 with chronological parallel Revelation 6 and Matthew 24 verses have the elect as those who live through the great tribulation.

3) Revelation 12:10–11 says "the accuser of our brothers (Satan) has been thrown down… And they have conquered him by the blood of the Lamb and by the word of their testimony, for they loved not their lives even unto death."

4) Revelation 12:17 has "those who keep the commandments of God and hold to the testimony of Jesus."

Sometimes pretribulation proponents will use the Philadelphia church of Revelation 3:7–13 to claim the eschatological church will be raptured before the seventieth week. They key in on verse 10 which has this church being kept from the hour of trial. There are several problems. First, the Greek word for rapture harpazó cannot be found in this Scripture. Second, the verse 10 Greek verb *tērēsō* is from *téreó*, which is to watch over, to guard. The same Greek verb can be found in John 17:15, which confirms it does not mean removal from the earth, though more of a physical protection from the evil one while on earth.

> I do not ask that you take them out of the world, but that *you keep them* (Greek *tērēsēs*) from the evil one. (John 17:15, emphasis added)

> Because you have kept my word about patient endurance, I *will keep* (Greek *tērēsō*) you from the hour of trial that is coming on the whole world, to try those who dwell on the earth. (Rev. 3:10, emphasis added)

Third, there is only one group who are promised protection during the great tribulation. The promised group are the Jewish remnant in Israel who flee as commanded in the Old Testament of Zechariah 14:5 (cf. Matt. 24:15–20) will be granted relief (2 Thess. 1:7). The woman (Israel) will be provided protection for three and a half years (Rev. 12:13–16), though the church is not promised any protection in verse 17 when the great tribulation starts. After the great tribulation the church (elect) will be raptured as evident by Revelation 7:9–17, though before that same day "day of the Lord."

FIFTH PRETRIB PROBLEM – MARTYRS CRYING OUT

Those under the altar who are killed for their righteous faith ask the Lord in Revelation 6:10, "How long before you will judge and avenge our blood on those who dwell on the earth." Those slain righteous ones are saying the Lord has not yet responded for their death; therefore, God's worldwide judgment against the wicked has not yet begun. Since they are martyred in the fifth opened seal (Rev. 6:9–11), which starts the second half of the seventieth prophetic week, a rapture before this midpoint is not possible.

SIXTH – THREE UNIQUE THEOPANIES

Most pretribulation scholars overlook the significance of the unique theophanies found in Revelation 8:5, 11:19, and 16:18. A notable exception John MacArthur, who recognizes four theophanies (Rev. 4:5, 8:5, 11:19, and 16:18) should be viewed as manifestations of God's presence, rather than only the first.[3] It is worth noting that Revelation 4:5 is unique in not being accompanied by an earthquake, with its location in heaven.

Pastor John then categorizes the last three theophanies as expressions of "divine wrath," though he provides no supporting rationale for this classification. In contrast, beyond prewrath proposes that each represents a unique day of Christ (rapture) with their lightning and thunder.[4] The three earthly theophanies are as follows:

1) **Revelation 8:5:** This first theophany occurs during the opening of the seventh seal, pertaining to the faith-based church.

2) **Revelation 11:19:** This second theophany is associated with the blowing of the seventh trumpet, primarily for the faith-based Jewish people who must be spiritually saved after the church's rapture.

3) **Revelation 16:18:** The final theophany appears during the pouring of the seventh bowl, directed towards the works-based "sheep" described in Matthew 25:31–46.

From the throne came *flashes of lightning, and rumblings and peals of thunder,* and before the throne were burning seven torches of fire, which are the seven spirits of God, and before the throne there was as it were a sea of glass, like crystal. (Rev. 4:5–6, emphasis added)

Then the angel took the censer and filled it with fire from the altar and threw it on the earth, and there were *peals of thunder, rumblings, flashes of lightning, and an earthquake.* (Rev. 8:5, emphasis added)

---

3 John MacArthur, *The MacArthur New Testament Commentary Revelation 1–11*, Moody Publishers, 820 N. LaSalle Blvd., Chicago, IL 60610, © 1999, 151.

4 See chapter 5, third prewrath problem.

Then God's temple in heaven was opened, and the ark of his covenant was seen within his temple. There were *flashes of lightning, rumblings, peals of thunder, an earthquake, and heavy hail*. (Rev. 11:19, emphasis added)

And there were *flashes of lightning, rumblings, peals of thunder, and a great earthquake* such as there had never been since man was on the earth, so great was that earthquake. (Rev. 16:18, emphasis added)

SEVENTH – NO SCRIPTURE SUPPORTS IT

Overall, the pretribulation exegesis lacks explicit scriptural support for their assertion that the rapture will occur on or before the beginning of the seventieth week. In their book *Imminency*, Robert Van Kampen and Charles Cooper, prewrath scholars, aptly referred to this doctrine as *The Phantom Doctrine* in their subtitle, highlighting the lack of adequate scriptural backing for the pretribulation timing.[5]

Surprisingly, a few well recognized pretribulation proponents say that there is no Scripture that supports a rapture before the seventieth week or for other premillennial views during it.[6] The beyond prewrath does have an explicit Scripture for the earthly elect rapture in Revelation 8:5 theophany with the consequence being the rejoicing in heaven (Rev. 7:9–17).

THE SEVENTIETH WEEK IS NOT *THE TRIBULATION*

Many scholars, teachers, and seminary professors often refer to the entire seventieth week of Daniel as *The Tribulation*. However, this designation is incorrect for the following reasons.

First, Matthew 24:29 and its parallel in Revelation 6:12 indicate that the tribulation ends when the sixth seal is opened. Since the sixth seal is within

---

5   Robert Van Kampen and Charles Cooper, *Imminency The Phantom Doctrine*, Published by Sola Scriptura, P.O. Box 770, Grand Haven, MI 49417, © 2000.
6   Tim LaHaye, *No Fear of the Storm*, Multnomah Press Books and Questar Publishers, Inc., P.O. Box 1720, Sisters, OR 97759, © 1992, 69, 188; Hal Lindsey, *The Rapture*, The Aorist Corporation, © 1983, 32; and Mark Hitchcock, *The End*, Tyndale House Publishers, Inc., © 1992, 136.

the seventieth week, it is illogical to label the entire prophetic week as "The Tribulation," even if this particular seal lasts only one day. To then suggest that the entire prophetic week is merely a time of calamity introduces a definition not found in Scripture, complicating eschatological understanding unnecessarily.

> I said to him, "Sir, you know." And he said to me, "These are the ones coming out of the great tribulation. They have washed their robes and made them white in the blood of the Lamb. (Rev. 7:14)

Second, Revelation 6:7–8 explicitly labels the fourth opened seal as a tribulation, with its parallel in Matthew 24:9–14. The first three opened seals are identified as birth pangs, further supporting the notion that the entire seventieth week cannot be uniformly labeled as *The Tribulation*.

Third, Scripturally tribulation is considered persecution against those of faith (Matt. 24:21; John 16:33; Rom. 12:12) and not against the wicked.

RAPTURE NAMING SCHEMES ARE DECEPTIVE

The naming schemes for the pretribulation, midtribulation, and post-tribulation views can be misleading since they all imply that the seventieth week of Daniel is synonymous with *The Tribulation*. While it is true that simply assigning a name doesn't guarantee accuracy, it is crucial for students of eschatology to exercise discernment and critical thinking.

A more accurate naming scheme for the pretribulation view could have been something like "pre-seventieth week" or "pre-70." However, given the widespread familiarity with the existing naming conventions after many decades of use, it may be more practical to continue with these misleading labels.

MASSIVE REVIVAL AT MIDPOINT

The pretribulation view is correct in suggesting, or at least implying, that a massive revival will occur during the seventieth week. The worldwide proclamation of God's word, as depicted in the first angel's announcement in Revelation 14:6–7 (cf. Matt. 24:14), highlights this reality. This event takes place on the very day the great tribulation begins, if not moments before, coinciding with the abomination of desolation at the midpoint (Matt. 24:15;

cf. Dan. 9:27). This does not pose a beyond prewrath challenge, as seven pretribulation issues have been addressed earlier.

SHEEP: WORKS-BASED VS FAITH-BASED

A distinction can be made between the *works-based* sheep (Matt. 25:35–36) and the *faith-based* sheep (v. 46b). Scripture consistently affirms that salvation is by faith, not by works (Eph. 2:8–9).

1) **Works-based:** These sheep are described as "blessed by my Father" and are separated from the goats based on their works (Matt. 25:34–36). They are believed to populate the earth during the millennial reign of Jesus.

2) **Faith-based:** These sheep are referred to as "righteous," inheriting eternal life (v. 46b), consistent with the doctrine of salvation by faith.

How, then, can these seemingly opposing passages be reconciled for the same sheep? The following paragraphs offer one possible harmonization. Regardless of the interpretive approach, there is a strong case that these "sheep" represent those who will be reigned over during the millennium and constitute a third dispensational group—a distinct people of God.

The works-based sheep are taken based on at least one of six acts of kindness to Jesus's brothers (Matt. 12:50, 25:35–36). They appear to be those taken in Revelation 16:18 theophany, having missed the *bema seat* judgment described in Revelation 11:18, as expected. These individuals may later be identified as the wedding guests at the marriage feast (Matt. 22:1–14; Rev. 19:9–10).

It may be at this feast—upon seeing Christ in His glory—that they profess Him as Lord and Savior, thereby receiving faith-based eternal life. However, they would not receive their glorified, eternal bodies until after inheriting "the kingdom prepared for you" (Matt. 25:34). During the millennium, they would live long but still mortal lives, eventually experiencing physical death (Isa. 65:19–25). They seem to serve as witnesses to their descendants during this period.

It is not until the arrival of the new earth that death is finally abolished (Isa. 65:17–18; Rev. 21:1–4).

CONCLUSION

The critique of the pretribulation claim for a rapture before the seventieth week of Daniel rests on seven reasons, with the first three and the sixth by this author being particularly novel. First, the beyond prewrath assertion that Jesus's parousia, from heaven to earth, occurs at the midpoint of the seventieth week renders an earlier pretribulation rapture untenable. Essentially, Jesus's parousia from heaven to earth, must coincide or precede with the elect rapture for coherence. Pretribulation fail to recognize that the elect rapture is accompanied by the world seeing Jesus (Matt. 24:30–31; Rev. 1:7), which must be considered a presence (parousia) of Jesus.

Second, the absence of a multitude rejoicing in heaven in Revelation 4, where a pretribulation rapture is often placed, stands in contrast to expectations. Third, pretribulation proponents have Jesus returning, from heaven to earth, on a white horse for the Armageddon battle, though Jesus did not ascend into heaven on a horse. Jesus must return the way he left (Acts 1:9–11), which is on foot.

Fourth, most pretribulation scholars do not recognize the significance of the theophanies in Revelation 4:5, 8:5, 11:19, and 16:18. John MacArthur acknowledges that all these instances represent the presence of God. However, Pastor John further categorizes them as expressions of "divine wrath." In contrast, beyond prewrath interprets the last three theophanies as distinct rapture events with their thunder and lightning, which is almost always associated with the righteous and not the wicked.

In summary, there is no scriptural support for a pretribulation rapture preceding the onset of the seventieth week of Daniel.

Chapter 4

Harpazó and Prewrath

PURPOSE

This chapter aims to explore the meaning of the Greek word *harpazó*, followed by an overview of the original perspectives of two prewrath authors.

HARPAZÓ

Harpazó from the Greek translation means a snatching away of believers considered to be a rapture. Surprisingly, its only occurrence in the book of Revelation is in 12:5 where it describes Jesus alone being taken to heaven. One might expect this term to appear more frequently in a book primarily focused on end-times events. As a result, premillennial exegesis is unable to support precise timing using harpazó within the structured framework of Revelation, with its seven seals, seven trumpets, and seven bowls.

The figure below illustrates the chronological parallels between Matthew 24 and Revelation 6 and 8 from the beyond prewrath perspective.

> She gave birth to a male child, one who is to rule all the nations with a rod of iron, but her child was *caught up* (Greek *harpazó*) to God and to his throne. (Rev. 12:5, emphasis added)

FIGURE 8: MATT. 24 AND REV. 6–8 PARALLELS

Matthew 24	Parallels	Revelation 6, 8
vv. 4–5	Peaceful conquest (birth pangs)	Opened seal 1 (6:1–2)
vv. 6–7	Wars (birth pangs)	Opened seal 2 (6:3–4)
v. 7	Famines and earthquakes (birth pangs)	Opened seal 3 (6:5–6)
vv. 9–14	Death and tribulation (hard labor)	Opened seal 4 (6:7–8)
vv. 15–28	Jesus's and Satan's coming, martyrdom and great tribulation (hard labor)	Opened seal 5 (6:9–11)
v. 29	"Wrath of the Lamb" (no tribulation)	Opened seal 6 (6:12–17)
vv. 30–31, 37–42	Normal life, then rapture (Day of Christ) (no tribulation)	Opened seal 7 (8:1–5)
vv. 37–42	Wrath of God	Blown trumpet 1 (8:7)

CLASSIC PREWRATH

Prewrath is a good premillennial view created by Marvin Rosenthal and Robert Van Kampen, which this author previously held to.

PREWRATH BY MARVIN ROSENTHAL

In 1990, Marvin Rosenthal published *The Pre-Wrath Rapture of the Church*. This was the first book to promote this premillennial view.

He has labeled both the fifth and sixth seals as the great tribulation with the rapture occurring after this. Prewrath has the Revelation 7:9–17 multitude rejoicing in heaven as the scriptural location of the associated earthly rapture. This sequential interpretation is seen in Scripture with it located after Revelation 6:12–17, the sixth opened seal, though before Revelation 8:1–5 with its seventh opened seal. The figure below depicts Marvin's prewrath representation.[1]

---

1   Marvin Rosenthal, *The Pre-wrath Rapture of the Church* (Nashville: Thomas Nelson, 1990), 211.

FIGURE 9: PREWRATH BY MARVIN ROSENTHAL

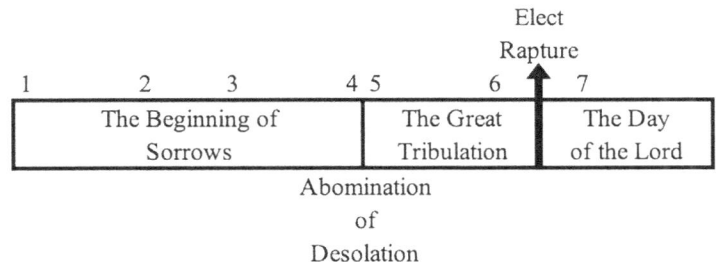

PRE-WRATH BY ROBERT VAN KAMPEN

In 1992, Robert Van Kampen published *The Sign of Christ's Coming and the End of the Age*, which was the second book to promote the prewrath premillennial rapture located in Revelation 7:9–17, which defines it. The figure below represents Robert Van Kampen's prewrath depiction from his book.[2]

Van Kampen's perspective differs from Marvin Rosenthal's in that he places the great tribulation also within the context of the fourth seal. Additionally, Van Kampen introduces the concept of "Israel Saved" at the conclusion of the seventieth week of Daniel. It remains ambiguous in Van Kampen's book whether he intended for Israel to be spiritually, physically, or both saved at that moment. He does not explicitly use the word "rapture" in reference to Israel, making this distinction unclear.

---

2   Robert Van Kampen, *The Sign of Christ's Coming and the End of the Age* (Wheaton, IL: Crossway Books, 1992), 410.

FIGURE 10: PREWRATH BY ROBERT VAN KAMPEN

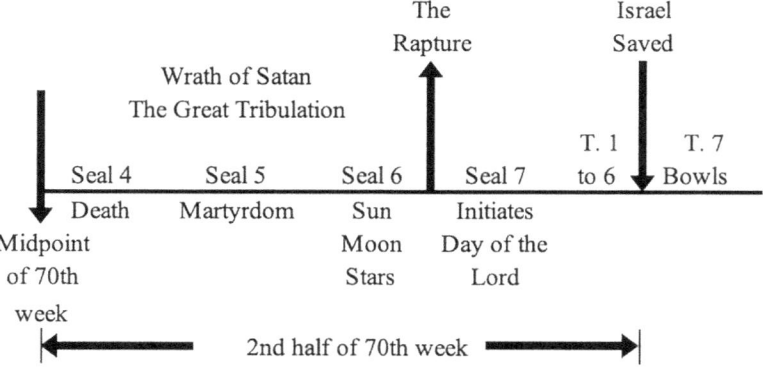

CONCLUSION

The Greek word *harpazó*, from which we derive the term "rapture," cannot be utilized by any premillennial view to precisely locate its occurrence relative to the events described in the seven opened seals and seven blown trumpets. However, the Greek word *parousia* for coming, found in Matthew 24:27, offers valuable chronological guidance regarding the coming of Jesus, later discussed in chapter 6, seventh chronological reason.

In this discussion, we explored the classic prewrath perspective presented by Robert Van Kampen and Marvin Rosenthal. Prewrath asserts that Jesus's coming, as described in Matthew 24:27, occurs after the great tribulation and is associated with the consequence of the church rapture, where believers will gather with Jesus in the sky on the same day as the day of the Lord. Robert Van Kampen's unique exegesis includes the concept of "Israel saved" at the end of the seventieth week, although it remains unclear whether his proposed salvation is physical, spiritual, or both in nature.

Chapter 5

Prewrath Problems – Part 1

PURPOSE

This chapter serves to outline a series of agreements between prewrath and beyond prewrath perspectives before delving into identifying prewrath problems. While six of these issues are discussed within this chapter, one based on chronology will be explored in the next chapter.

Beyond prewrath draws from elements of midtribulation, prewrath, and posttribulation positions, yet it represents a distinctly different premillennial stance. Without the groundwork laid by these scholars, the development of beyond prewrath would be improbable.

It is important to note that the author does not assert the prophetic truth of all beyond prewrath exegesis, nor should any one claim their prophetic exegesis to be infallibly accurate. As Daniel 9:24 reminds us, all prophecy remains unknown until the end of the seventieth week. Nevertheless, this should not deter efforts to understand this prophetic mystery. New interpretations of Scripture should be proposed and examined to determine their potential merit.

BEYOND PRE-WRATH BY ROBERT PARKER

In 2021, Robert Parker released *Beyond Prewrath End-Time Prophecy*, which was later expanded in the following year. This work presented the concept of beyond prewrath eschatology, offering a distinctive perspective on end-time prophecy.

The figure below illustrates the beyond prewrath interpretation of the elect rapture occurring within the context of the seventh opened seal, alongside a day of the Lord associated with the first blown trumpet, both taking place on the same day.

FIGURE 11: BEYOND PREWRATH TIMELINE

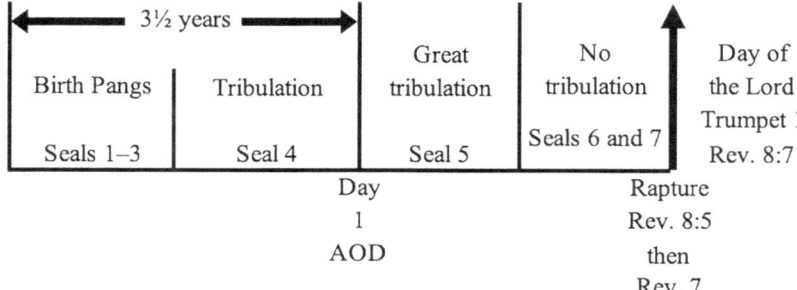

AGREEMENTS

The following are agreements with the prewrath and beyond prewrath.

1) In Revelation 7:9–17, the multitude rejoicing in heaven are the elect who came out of the great tribulation.

2) A day of the Lord occurs after and on the same day as the church rapture.

3) Israel must endure through all seventy prophetic weeks of Daniel.

4) The seven blown trumpets and seven poured bowls are a wrath of God.

5) The elect (church) rapture occurs after the great tribulation, though before the blown trumpet judgments.

6) There are precursor events (first five seals and two in 2 Thess. 2:1–4) to the elect rapture, which prevent the pretribulation any moment rapture.

7) Most, if not all, prewrath scholars would agree the Holy Spirit is not taken with the elect rapture.

SEVEN PREWRATH PROBLEMS

There are seven prewrath categorized problems. From this the beyond prewrath dispensational solution provides robust exegesis, presenting a new premillennial view.

FIRST PROBLEM: JESUS'S PAROUSIA AT THE MIDPOINT

The first issue with the prewrath perspective is its failure to recognize Jesus's parousia, from heaven to earth, at the midpoint, particularly on the Mt. of Olives. This event, as discussed in chapter 1, is significant and opens the possibility of another gathering and a day of the Lord earlier than the prewrath interpreted elect rapture day. By not acknowledging this aspect, prewrath interpretations overlook important nuances in the timing and nature of end-time events.

MATTHEW 24:36–39, UNKNOWN DAY AND HOUR

Many believe that pinpointing the exact day and hour of Jesus's return from heaven to earth is impossible, referencing Matthew 24:36. They assume that Jesus's return will coincide with a simultaneous rapture. However, this author argues they are distinct chronological events. Pretrib proponents agree they are different chronological events, though in reverse order.

First, verses 37–39 clarify that the concept of knowing that "day and hour" relates to the analogy of distinguishing between the righteous and the wicked, similar to the prophecies given to Lot and Noah. Second, Chapter 1 previously indicated that Jesus returns from heaven to earth at the midpoint of the prophetic timeline. Revelation 7:9–17, which describes rejoicing in heaven following the opening of the fifth and sixth seals, suggests that the rapture of the church occurs after this midpoint.

Third, the Greek term *parousia* can refer to either a coming, from heaven to earth or a continuous presence. This ongoing presence should be understood as a series of events, rather than a single occurrence. Reflective of Jesus first parousia as a series of events, e.g., birth, ministry, crucifixion, and resurrection. Eschatology it includes, but is not limited to, the battles of Jerusalem, Jehoshaphat, and Armageddon. Fourth, there is no scriptural basis for the idea that the exact day of Jesus's return from heaven to earth must coincide with a simultaneous rapture.

Therefore, Jesus's return to earth at the midpoint—1,260 days (half of a prophetic week, as per Dan. 9:27) after the prince strengthens the covenant—can be considered a knowable day event. This is distinct from the later, unknown exact day of the elect's rapture mentioned in Matthew 24:36.

But concerning that day and hour (when the righteous are taken) no one knows, not even the angels of heaven, nor the Son, but the Father only. For as were the days of Noah, so will be the coming of the Son of Man. (Matt. 24:36–37)

SECOND PROBLEM: GATHERINGS AND DAYS OF THE LORD

Another issue with the prewrath perspective is its interpretation of 2 Thessalonians 2:1 where "our gathering" is seen as a consequence of a rapture event. However, neither the Greek word harpazó for rapture, nor meeting Jesus in the sky can be explicitly found in this passage. The prewrath view derives this interpretation but fails to recognize that there are at least two different pairs of gatherings, each with an associated same-day "day of the Lord," which prevents an immediate placement to an elect rapture event without proper analysis. Three chronological pairs are proposed, as previously discussed in chapter 1. The chronological placement of 2 Thessalonians 2 should be reconsidered earlier, as at the midpoint.

a. Matthew 24:17–20 describes the first gathering of those on their Jerusalem housetops. Beyond prewrath places this with Jesus's return, from heaven to earth, in verse 27 to the Mt. of Olives (Zech. 14:4), suggesting a gathering, though not with all in the sky as a consequence of a rapture. The day of the Lord is represented in Zechariah 14:1. Chapter 1 supported this as at the midpoint with 2 Thessalonians 1 and 2.

b. Matthew 24:30–31 describes a later gathering of the elect to meet Jesus in the sky, as indicated in 1 Thessalonians 4:16–17 and Revelation 1:7, representing a rapture event. The rapture is represented in Revelation 8:5 theophany and the same day "day of the Lord" in verse 7.

c. Revelation 19:9 to 20:3 describes a proposed third pair. The Armageddon battle, which is a gathering of the righteous (Jesus and bride of Christ) battling against the wicked on their day of the Lord.

THIRD PROBLEM: THREE UNIQUE THEOPHANIES

The third prewrath problem lies in their failure to recognize the significance of the phrase "peals of thunder, rumblings, flashes of lightning, and an earthquake." This author identifies three scripturally unique phrases as constituting three great dispensational theophanies. While the word sequence may vary slightly across different passages, the content remains consistent.

A similarly unique theophany is found in Revelation 4:5–11, though it lacks the earthquake mentioned in the three other passages. This theophany emanates from the throne of God in heaven. When the same phrase is encountered later in Revelation (8:5, 11:19, 16:18) with an earthquake, it should be interpreted as indicative of the presence of God.

John MacArthur's *New Testament Commentary of Revelation* supports this interpretation. However, he further categorizes these three theophanies as "divine wrath," without explicitly discussing his reasoning.[1] Beyond prewrath disagrees. The theophanies are distinct in their use of thunder and lightning, which is almost always associated with the righteous, not the wicked (Ex. 19:16–20; Job 36:32; 2 Kings 2:11; Hab. 3:11; Luke 17:24–26; 1 Thess. 4:17). Satan's coming is only "like" lightning in Luke 10:18.

The beyond prewrath position points to Revelation 8:7, which describes "hail and fire mixed with blood," as representing the "fire and sulfur" prophecy in Luke 17:29. According to Luke 17:27 and 17:29, before this wrath is directed at the wicked, the righteous will be physically separated from it, as seen in the cases of Lot and Noah. The theophany in Revelation 8:5, which occurs before the wrath events described in verse 7, appears to symbolize the separation of the righteous and suggests their rapture (day of Christ) rather than divine wrath against the wicked. These two scriptures, just two verses apart, supports the Luke 17 dual prophecy (physical saving of righteous and wrath of God) occurring on the same day, akin to the experiences of Lot and Noah. This interpretation of the Revelation 8:5 theophany as a rapture then supports the view that the later two theophanies (Rev. 11:19, 16:18) are also associated with a day of Christ.

---

1   John MacArthur, *The MacArthur New Testament Commentary Revelation 1–11*, Moody Publishers, 820 N. LaSalle Blvd., Chicago, IL 60610, © 1999, 151.

1) First Great Dispensational Theophany: Revelation 8:5 theophany pertains to the church rapture to heaven.

2) Second Great Dispensational Theophany: Revelation 11:19 theophany relates mostly, if not completely, to the Jewish people, with their rapture likely occurring immediately before the béma, likely to Jerusalem. The beyond prewrath dispensational rapture of the Jewish saints has parallels with the posttribulation view of the rapture at the end of the seventieth week.

3) Third Great Dispensational Theophany: Revelation 16:18 theophany is interpreted as pertaining to the sheep who are separated in the sheep and goat judgment outlined in Matthew 25:31–45. In this judgment, those deemed "blessed by my Father" (v. 40) are identified by their assistance to Jesus's brothers through six acts of kindness listed in verses 35–36. These works-based criteria support the notion that the sheep will be subjects to be reigned over rather than part of the faith-based bride of Christ during the millennium.

LIGHTNING FLASHES WITHIN THE THEOPHANY

Indeed, lightning flashes within each theophany seem to signify the means by which each dispensational raptured group is forcibly taken. Both the church and Israel represent the bride of Christ, who will attend the béma in Revelation 11:18, despite each having a separate earthly rapture theophany. Lightning and its synonyms can be found in the following Scriptures.

1) Luke 17:24 says "…as lightning flashes…so will the return of the son of God be in his day." These lightning flashes are first seen at Jesus's coming in Matthew 24:27 at the midpoint, though not for a church rapture. The great tribulation does not end until verse 29.

2) Habakkuk 3:11 says "…the light of your arrows as they sped…"

3) Job 36:32 says, "He covers his hands with lightning and commands it to strike the mark."

4) Elijah was separated from Elisha with "chariots of fire," which is a lightning metaphor. 2 Kings 2:11, then taken in a whirlwind. "Chariots of horses" seem to indicate a fast-moving event. Exodus 9:24, 28 equates fire and lightning, which is common in the Old Testament.

5) After and perhaps during the lightning flashes believers seem to be transformed into imperishable bodies to meet the Son of Man (Jesus) in the clouds-sky (Matt. 24:30–31; 1 Cor. 15:50–54).

THUNDER WITHIN THE THEOPHANY

In Genesis 3:8, Yahweh is described as moving through the garden of Eden with the wind of the storm. In Exodus 19:18–20, during Israel's first exodus into the Sinai, the Lord's presence was accompanied by thunder when he answered Moses. Additionally, there was an earthquake, smoke, and a loud trumpet noise that grew louder and louder.

FOURTH GROUP – SURVIVE INTO MILLENNIUM

There appears to be a fourth group separate from the earlier three rapture groups (Rev. 8:5, 11:19, 16:18), as indicated in Daniel 12:12. This fourth group is not raptured, though endures on earth until Day 1,335, which marks the beginning of the millennium.[2] Isaiah 24:1 depicts the earth as being made desolate of humans, though verse 6 adds clarification that this is hyperbole since a few do survive to Day 1,335. These few survivors can be characterized by:

1) They never accepted Jesus as their Lord and Savior, as evidenced by their absence from the earlier raptures mentioned in Revelation 8:5 or 11:19 theophanies.

2) They never showed any of the six acts of works-based kindness to Jesus's brothers (church or Jewish people) outlined in Matthew 25:35–36, as they were not raptured in Revelation 16:18.

Some, if not all, of the ten beasts (Dan. 7:24) will somehow survive into the millennium, though their dominion or kingdom will be taken away. These beasts will only live for a time and a season (total of fifteen months) from when the beast was killed (Dan. 7:11–12). There could be others not

---

2 Providing support for this 1,335 day start of the millennium are: Robert Van Kampen in the *Sign of Christ's Coming and the End of the Age* as evident on his page 463 illustration, Marvin Rosenthal in *The Pre-wrath Rapture of the Church* on his page 276 illustration, and Robert Parker's *Beyond Prewrath End-Time Prophecy* as evident on his page 145 illustration.

explicitly identified in Scripture who could also make it into the start of the thousand-year reign of Jesus. The man of lawlessness, considered "the beast," will be captured in Revelation 19:19–20 and thrown into hades though before the millennium starts.

> I looked then because of the sound of the great words that the horn was speaking. And as I looked, the beast (man of lawlessness) was killed, and its body destroyed and given over to be burned with fire. As for the rest of the beasts, their dominion was taken away, but their lives were prolonged for a season and a time. (Dan. 7:11–12)

FOURTH PROBLEM: WICKED DESTROYED WITH FIRE

The fourth issue with the prewrath perspective is that the prophecy in Luke 17:29 of "fire and brimstone" against the wicked cannot be found in the seventh opened seal of Revelation 8:1–5, which sequentially follows the multitude rejoicing in heaven in Revelation 7:9–17, a sequence that beyond prewrath considers non-chronological.

The prewrath interpretation suggests that the day of the Lord begins in Revelation 8:1 with the "silence in heaven," which does not explicitly imply death. Only when Scripture progresses to verse 7, with "hail and fire mixed with blood," do they find a description of death. While eschatological death by water, as with the flood during Noah's time, is possible, it is not depicted as a means to destroy all flesh (Gen. 9:11; cf. 2 Peter 2:4–10).

Prewrath and beyond prewrath agree this day of the Lord must occur on the same day as the elect rapture but after it. Also, this same day sequential event is supported by Luke 17:28–34, which references Noah and Lot.

Beyond prewrath says the expected rapture verse must precede Revelation 8:7, which must describe an interpreted day of the Lord. Since the sixth seal entails twenty-four-hour darkness, it strongly suggests that the seventh seal of Revelation 8:1–5 occurs during a normal daytime-nighttime cycle, likely when the rapture would take place.[3] Beyond prewrath identifies verse 5, with its theophany, as the moment of the elect rapture, labeled as the first great dispensational theophany. Therefore, Revelation 7, with the arrival of the 144,000 from the twelve Hebrew tribes on earth and the church rejoicing in heaven separately, is the consequence of the derived dispensational elect rapture depicted in Revelation 8:5 theophany.

---

3   See chapter 6.

FIFTH: NEED TO ACCOUNT FOR ISRAEL REMNANT

The fifth prewrath problem is that the majority of these scholars do not adequately account for the Israel remnant when their 1,260 days of nourishment and protection ends in Revelation 12:14. It seems incongruous for the Lord to protect the Jewish remnant for an exact 1,260 days and then cease protection during the seven poured bowls when there is still danger of persecution from the Antichrist. Additionally, Daniel 9:24 decrees that the Jewish people must live through all seventy prophetic weeks of Daniel, which together point to their rapture on the exact day when their last prophetic week is complete with the seventh blown trumpet. This last verse is Revelation 11:19 with its theophany, labeled as the second great dispensational theophany, is proposed as a rapture.

The exception to this prewrath disagreement is Robert Van Kampen in *The Sign of Christ's Coming and the End of the Age*, who does appear to account for the Israel remnant being saved before their 1,260 days of protection are over. However, he does not distinguish whether it is spiritual salvation, physical rapture, or perhaps both on the same day. He interprets the 1,260 days ending in the sixth blown trumpet, rather than the seventh, as posited in beyond prewrath.

The completion of the two witnesses' testimony in Revelation 11:7, followed by their death in verse 8, supports the beyond prewrath Jewish chronology of spiritual salvation just before the witnesses' death. At least three and a half days later (vv. 7–11), the witnesses are taken to heaven in verse 12. Then the seventh trumpet is blown in verse 15. A deduced physical rapture of the Jewish people in verse 19 theophany follows, as expected, with the witnesses's previous prophetic mission completion of spiritual salvation. However, the Jewish people are not likely taken to heaven at that moment, as the second rejoicing in heaven is not depicted until eight chapters later (Rev. 11:19 Jewish rapture verses 19:1–5 rejoicing). They would be attending the béma with Revelation 11:18, likely in Jerusalem.

In summary, Israel cannot be raptured with the church for at least three reasons. Firstly, they must remain on earth until the seventieth week is complete, fulfilling the prophecy of seventy prophetic weeks decreed for them in Daniel 9:24–25. Secondly, they are not spiritually saved until the sixth blown trumpet, which occurs after the church is raptured in the seventh opened seal. Thirdly, their spiritual salvation must occur at or before the two witnesses mission is completed in the sixth blown trumpet with their death and resurrection.

ISRAEL MOURNS AT THE FIRST RAPTURE

The mourning of the tribes (Jewish people) in Revelation 1:7 when all will see Jesus, represented as a church rapture, poses a challenge for many prewrath scholars who do not account for this event. If the tribes had been spiritually saved earlier and then raptured with the church, they would not be mourning but rejoicing with the church in heaven. This supports the timing of Israel's spiritual salvation, as indicated in Acts 2:21, occurring chronologically after the elect rapture in Revelation 8:5 theophany.

> Behold, he is coming with the clouds, and every eye will see him, even those who pierced him, and all tribes of the earth will wail on account of him. Even so. Amen. (Rev. 1:7)

SIXTH, PART 1: SHEEP – NOT ACCOUNTED FOR

Another significant issue with the prewrath perspective is its failure to account for the works-based sheep mentioned in the sheep and goat judgment of Matthew 25:31–46, who inherit the kingdom and are deduced to be the subjects being reigned over. The sheep are taken in Revelation 16:18 during the seventh poured bowl. Their rapture would not entail an immortal body but rather a seemingly new mortal body, as they become the subjects who enjoy long lives in the millennium kingdom but eventually face physical death (Isa. 65:20). Death will not be any more until after the millennium, when there is a new earth and new heavens (Rev. 21:4; cf. Isa. 65:17–18).

Scripturally, being raptured does not necessarily imply eternal salvation with an eternal body. Context is crucial. For instance, the apostle Philip was raptured to another location on earth after baptizing the eunuch in Acts 8:39–40, yet he later experienced physical death.

During the great tribulation, those beheaded for Jesus (Rev. 20:4) are prophesied to reign with Christ for a thousand years over the subjects. It would not make sense for them and the twelve apostles (Luke 22:28–30) to reign-judge over other believers with eternal bodies who were raptured and resurrected. Therefore, the works-based sheep of Matthew 25:31–46 must be understood as the subjects being reigned over.

Matthew 25:34 indicates that the sheep are "blessed by the Father" and are invited to "inherit the kingdom prepared for you from the foundation of the world." This kingdom refers to the millennium when Jesus reigns on earth. The criteria to inherit this kingdom is based on works and not faith, indicating that the sheep will experience physical death during the millennium. This works-based group likely represents the wedding guests who attend the marriage supper in Revelation 19:9–10. The rapture criteria for the bride of Christ who attend the earlier béma is different, based on being saved through faith (Eph. 2:8–9).

1) "I was hungry and you gave me food (works-based)" (Matt. 25:35).
2) "I was thirsty and you gave me drink (works-based)" (Matt. 25:35; cf. Mark 9:41).
3) "I was a stranger and you welcomed me (works-based)" (Matt. 25:35).
4) "I was naked and you clothed me (works-based)" (Matt. 25:36).
5) "I was sick and you visited me (works-based)" (Matt. 25:36).
6) "I was in prison and you came to me (works-based)" (Matt. 25:36).

SIXTH, PART 2: SHEEP – SOME MUST BE JEWISH

When Israel, from their Revelation 11:19 rapture, attends the béma in 11:18 they are each individually given their rewards and thus counted. God promised Abraham and his descendants in Genesis 15:5 to be as numerous as the stars in heaven. King David tried to count them in 1 Chronicles 21, which was a sin.

The twice daily temple sacrifices in the millennium require Levite priests (Ezek. 44:15–46:24) who will be determined by the LORD (Isa. 66:21). These Jewish priests must be considered to be some of the works-based sheep, who are being reigned over, to keep the exact number of Abraham descendants unknown until at least the great white throne at the end of Jesus's thousand-year reign. During the thousand years, Abraham descendants as part of the sheep will live long lives and have offspring, which helps keep the Jewish exact population count unknown until then.

> And he (a vision of the LORD) brought him (Abram) outside and said, "Look toward heaven, and number the stars, if you are able to number them." Then he said to him, "So shall your offspring be." (Gen. 15:5)

SEVENTH PROBLEM: CHRONOLOGICAL

Prewrath chronological misinterpretations are discussed in chapter 6.

CONCLUSION

This chapter summarizes the main points of contention with the prewrath perspective and outlines how the beyond prewrath position addresses these issues. It highlights the unique contributions of the beyond prewrath view, particularly in its interpretation of theophanies, the protection of the Israel remnant, the timing of the day of the Lord, the inclusion of the works-based sheep from the sheep and goat judgment, and the recognition of Jesus's parousia from heaven to earth at the midpoint. Additionally, it emphasizes the need for a careful analysis of Scripture to understand the timing and nature of end-time events. Overall, it provides a clear and concise overview of the beyond prewrath position.

Jesus's coming (Greek noun *parousia*) is by definition both the day of his return and his continued presence. Jesus return, from heaven to earth, is seen as a knowable day at the midpoint. Jesus's continued presence will include the elect rapture at an unknown day and hour (Matt. 24:36–37).

Chapter 6

Prewrath Problems – Part 2

PURPOSE

The chronological issues within the prewrath perspective and the corresponding interpretation from the beyond prewrath viewpoint sets a clear foundation for understanding the differences between the two positions. By addressing the sequence of events in Revelation chapters 6 to 8, Matthew 24:27–31, and reconciling them with the timing of Jesus's coming and the elect rapture, a comprehensive analysis is presented that highlights the distinct features of the beyond prewrath perspective.

SEVENTH PROBLEM: SEVEN CHRONOLOGY REASONS

The seventh prewrath problem is they interpret Revelation chapters 6 to 8 as chronological. Beyond prewrath does not have them as chronological, i.e., sixth seal (Rev. 6:12–17), then seventh seal (Rev. 8:1–5) with the verse 5 theophany representing the proposed elect rapture, next rejoicing in heaven (Rev. 7:9–17), and on the same day as the rapture is a day of Lord in Revelation 8:7 when the first trumpet is blown. Basically, in Revelation 7:9–17 the multitude in heaven rejoicing must be interpreted as a consequence of the earthly rapture theophany of Revelation 8:5. There are seven reasons which help to support this chronological exegesis.

FIRST REASON – WRATH OF THE LAMB

A key chronological aspect is the nature of the wrath of the Lamb, which is distinct from causing death. In Revelation 6:12–17, the sixth opened seal depicts people hiding in caves and among the rocks, seemingly paralleling Isaiah 2:19–20 where individuals flee to caves and discard their idols. This indicates that those affected are likely the wicked. Since the fulfillment of this prophecy in Isaiah has not occurred, it is understood to be eschatological.

This event can be regarded as a relatively mild manifestation of the day of the Lord, as there is no explicit mention of death specifically targeted against the wicked—only mental anguish. Verses 15–17 depict individuals requesting rocks to fall on them, yet there is no indication that God grants this request. While there may be deaths from worldwide tsunamis caused by the great earthquake of Revelation 6:12, these casualties would affect anyone living in coastal regions, not just the wicked.

Additionally, Isaiah 2:6–11, 17 suggests that the casting away of idols and the humbling of individuals before God are associated with this event. This implies that those who were previously controlled by idols are no longer under their influence, at least temporarily, until later in the trumpet judgments when the wicked are seen returning to their idolatrous practices (Rev. 9:20–21). Despite expecting physical harm during this prolonged darkness, the wicked are not harmed, indicating a temporary and dramatic shift in their circumstances. The seventh seal, it is deduced, marks the beginning of a return to a normal day-night cycle, during which the wicked resume activities, such as marriages, planting, and building.

> So man is humbled, and each one is brought low— do not forgive them! (Isa. 2:9)

> And the haughtiness of man shall be humbled, and the lofty pride of men shall be brought low. (Isa. 2:17a)

> And the idols shall utterly pass away (Antichrist has temporarily lost control). And people shall enter the caves of the rocks. (Isa. 2:18–19a)

SECOND REASON – CELESTIAL DISTURBANCES

The celestial disturbances of Acts 2:17–21 is often interpreted by prewrath proponents as applicable to the church rapture occurring within the context of the sixth seal in Revelation 6:12–17. Some commentators and this author disagree and argue that the events described in Acts 2:14 to 5:42 are primarily focused on the Jewish audience of Peter's Pentecost sermon.[1] If this Jewish only interpretation is accepted, it would suggest that Acts 2:17–21 is not directly related to the church rapture and would, therefore, not be equated with the celestial disturbance described in Revelation 6:12–17. Beyond prewrath argues further that these events are distinct, as supported with figure 12 additional exegesis.

---

1   *ESV Study Bible*, Crossway, Wheaton, Illinois, www.crossway.org, © 2008, 2264.

In the second column, both sets of celestial disturbances involve twenty-four-hour darkness, which initially might not seem to differentiate them chronologically. In the third column, while Acts 2:17–21 speaks of death, this aspect is not explicitly mentioned in Revelation 6:12–17 as claimed by prewrath adherents.

In the fourth column, Revelation 6:12–17 includes an earthquake, which is absent in Acts 2:17–21. In the fifth column, Acts 2:17 speaks of God pouring out His Spirit on all flesh. This reference is absent in Revelation 6:12–17, which involves the wicked hiding in the rocks, contrasting with the righteous calling on the Lord as depicted in Acts 2:21.

FIGURE 12: DIFFERENT CELESTIAL DISTURBANCES

Scripture	Celestial Disturbances (24 hour darkness)	Death: Fire and blood	Earthquake	Everyone who calls on the Lord saved	When
Rev. 6:12–17	Yes	No	Yes	No	Sixth seal
Acts 2:17–21 and Joel 2:28–32	Yes	Yes	No	Yes	Sixth trumpet

An analysis of the use of darkness, blood, and fire with all twenty-one events (seven seals, seven trumpets, and seven bowls) provides additional support that Acts 2:17–21 is associated with the sixth blown trumpet and not the sixth opened seal. This was shown in chapter 2 of *Beyond Prewrath End-Time Prophecy.*

> *Immediately after the tribulation* of those days *the sun will be darkened* (twenty-four-hour darkness), and the moon will not give its light, and the stars will fall from heaven, and the *powers of the heavens will be shaken* (earthquake). (Matt. 24:29, emphasis added)

> When he opened the sixth seal, I looked, and behold, there was a great *earthquake*, and the *sun became black as sackcloth* (twenty-four-hour darkness), the full moon became like blood. (Rev. 6:12, emphasis added)

And it shall come to pass that everyone who calls upon the name of the Lord shall be saved. (Acts 2:21)

THIRD – MARRIAGES FORBIDDEN THEN ALLOWED

The third reason supporting the non-chronological interpretation of events in Revelation is the occurrence of marriages. Those who depart from the faith (2 Thess. 2:1–4, 10–12) are forbidden from marriage (1 Tim. 4:1–3), which was previously supported in figure 2 as before the midpoint. Later, according to Luke 17:27, marriages take place on the day of the elect rapture. However, during the sixth seal, characterized by twenty-four-hour darkness and people hiding in caves (Rev. 6:9–17; cf. Isa. 2:8–21), it is unlikely for marriages to occur, especially when the wicked are seeking death.

Therefore, marriages of those who have departed from the faith are more likely to happen later, during a normal day-night cycle, associated with the deduced seventh opened seal, which culminates with a rapture in Revelation 8:5 theophany. This suggests that the Antichrist's control over the wicked is temporarily ended during the sixth seal as the great tribulation ends, and this continues into the seventh seal.

> Now the Spirit expressly says that in later times some will depart from the faith by devoting themselves to deceitful spirits and teachings of demons, through the insincerity of liars whose consciences are seared, who *forbid marriage* and require abstinence from foods that God created to be received with thanksgiving by those who believe and know the truth. (1 Tim. 4:1–3, emphasis added)

> Just as it was in the days of Noah, so will it be in the days of the Son of Man. They were eating and drinking and *marrying and being given in marriage*, until the day when Noah entered the ark, and the flood came and destroyed them all. (Luke 17:26–27, emphasis added)

> The rest of mankind, who were not killed by these plagues, did not repent of the works of their hands nor give up worshiping demons and idols of gold and silver and bronze and stone and wood, which cannot see or hear or walk. (Rev. 9:20)

FOURTH REASON – REV. 8:1 DURATION

The fourth reason supporting the non-chronological interpretation of events in Revelation revolves around Revelation 8:1, which describes "silence in heaven for about half an hour." Prewrath scholars typically associate this silence with the beginning of the day of the Lord. However, the challenge arises from interpreting this half an hour in heaven as more than one earthly day, which contradicts the notion that the elect rapture and the day of the Lord occur on the same day.

The absence of "fire and sulfur" akin to Lot, in Revelation 8:1, where prewrath scholars place the start of the day of the Lord, is another issue. Instead, fire is mentioned later, in Revelation 8:7, which would fulfill Jesus's prophecy of Luke 17:29 as with Lot as proposed by beyond prewrath.

In the beyond prewrath perspective, Revelation 8:1's half an hour in heaven is considered equivalent to seven and a half days on earth. This conversion is based on a prophetic time ratio derived from the book of Daniel, which seems to find parallels with the timeframe mentioned before the flood in Noah's time. Genesis 7:4 and 7:10 indicate a period of seven days before the flood, which aligns closely with the derived seven and a half days of Revelation 8:1.[2] If this analogy holds true, it suggests that Revelation 8:1 encompasses more than one earthly day, which challenges the idea of the prewrath rapture occurring on the same day as with the day of the Lord.

FIFTH REASON – REV. 7:9–17 VERSUS 8:1

The chronological sequence in Revelation presents prewrath challenges when trying to determine the exact timing of events. Regarding the relationship between Revelation 7:9–17 and 8:1, several considerations arise:

1) Revelation 7:9 depicts a multitude in heaven holding palm branches, which suggests a celebratory atmosphere with physical bodies. The presence of these branches implies movement or interaction, potentially causing noise.

2) Revelation 7:10 describes loud rejoicing in heaven.

3) Revelation 7:13 mentions the multitude wearing white robes, which may also involve movement and generate sound.

---

2   Robert Parker, *Beyond Prewrath End-Time Prophecy,* © 2022, chapter 3.

Considering these factors, it seems unlikely that the events described in Revelation 7:9–17, characterized by physical activity and rejoicing, would chronologically occur before the silence described in Revelation 8:1. The transition from a jubilant celebration (Rev. 7:9–17) to sudden silence (Rev. 8:1) seems to be too abrupt and incongruous to happen in that order.

SIXTH REASON – SCRIPTURE NOT ALWAYS

The Bible itself provides instances where chronological order is not strictly followed, offering precedent for non-linear sequencing of events within its narratives. Two examples from the Old Testament illustrate this:

1) Jeremiah: Chapters 46–47 of the book of Jeremiah were written around 609 BC, while chapters 21–45, though chronologically later, are situated around 588 BC. This indicates that the arrangement of chapters in Jeremiah does not strictly adhere to chronological order.

2) Ezekiel: In the book of Ezekiel, we find instances where the events described do not follow a linear chronology. For example, Ezekiel 29:17 refers to an event occurring during the 27th year of Babylonian exile. However, subsequent verses in Ezekiel (such as 30:20, 31:1, 32:1, 7, 17, 33:21, and 40:1) describe events that took place in earlier years of the Babylonian exile, showcasing a non-linear arrangement of chronology.

These examples demonstrate that the Bible occasionally presents its content in a non-chronological manner, prioritizing thematic or theological considerations over strict chronology. Therefore, the possibility of non-chronological sequencing in Revelation, such as the juxtaposition of Revelation 7 and Revelation 8:1–5, is not unprecedented and should be considered within the broader context of biblical narrative structure.

SEVENTH REASON – MATTHEW 24:15–31

Beyond prewrath proposes Matthew 24:15–31 to describe three distinct chronological events related to the opening of seals five through seven, rather than the prewrath interpretation of four events (fifth, sixth, an interlude between sixth and seventh, and seventh seals). In biblical times, there was no such thing as an "interlude" between opening seals. Either one seal on the scroll is opened or the next. The prewrath chronological interpretation of the three Revelation 6–8 chapters is what leads to a misinterpretation.

The first event (Matt. 24:15–28), discussed previously in chapter 1, is proposed as Jesus's coming, from heaven to earth, at the midpoint. Matthew 24:27 (emphasis added) describes his coming with the imagery of "lightning *coming* (Greek noun *parousia*) from the east and shining as far as the west." This event seems associated with the gathering of those on their Jerusalem housetops (Matt. 24:17) who would witness King Jesus nearby on the Mt. of Olives (Isa. 33:17; Zech. 14:4), symbolizing the first of seven gatherings.

The second beyond prewrath event is described in Matthew 24:29 as twenty-four-hour darkness and an earthquake, which is parallel to the identified sixth opened seal of Revelation 6:12–17. The extended darkness helps to chronologically separate the fifth seal (Matt. 24:15–28 with derived light) from the seventh seal (Matt. 24:30–31 with its also derived light).

The third event is proposed to be associated with the seventh seal, with the gathering of the elect (Matt. 24:31) as a consequence of the earthly theophany described in Revelation 8:5, representing the elect rapture. Matthew 24:30 (emphasis added) says "they will see the Son of Man *coming* (Greek verb *erchomenon*) on the clouds of heaven," which is Jesus continued presence on earth (cf. Rev. 1:7).

This third event (Matt. 24:30–31) chronologically separated from the second event (Matt. 24:29) is deduced with Luke 17:28 (cf. Matt. 24:38–39) as analogous to Lot's situation when "they (the unrighteous) were ... planting and building." This parallels Jesus's analogy of Lot's family, representing the righteous, who were physically separated, lives saved, on the same day the wicked were destroyed. This aligns with the future elect rapture, where the righteous are physically separated with a rapture to the sky on the same day the wicked face destruction. Planting and building are daytime activities, contrasting with the twenty-four-hour darkness described in the second event.

Therefore, the elect rapture must occur after the extended darkness of the sixth seal to fulfill the prophecy of Lot's daytime activities. The same-day wrath of God, akin to Lot's situation, is proposed to occur in Revelation 8:7, the first blown trumpet, with its associated Sodom's fire, as prophesied by Jesus in Luke 17:29–30. This bounds the elect rapture to the seventh opened seal of Revelation 8:1–5, deduced to be verse 5 with its first of three dispensational earthly theophanies. The consequence of the earthly rapture will be gathering in the sky (Matt. 24:31) with the rejoicing (Rev. 7:9–17).

These reasons necessitate a chronological separation of the three sequential sets of verses: the fifth seal of Matthew 24:15–28 (great tribulation with a deduced normal day), followed by the sixth seal of verse 29 (twenty-four-hour darkness and no tribulation), and finally the seventh seal of verses 30–31 (deduced normal day with a rapture followed by the gathering of the elect in the sky and no tribulation).

FIGURE 13: FIFTH SEAL TO FIRST TRUMPET

Great tribulation Rev. 6:9–11 Light Seal 5	No tribulation Rev. 6:12–17 Darkness Seal 6	No tribulation Rev. 8:1–5 Light Seal 7	Day of the Lord Rev. 8:7 Trumpet 1
Midpoint Jesus's Parousia Matt. 24:27	Rev. 6:12 Matt. 24:29	Rapture Rev. 8:5 Matt. 24:30–31	

Likewise, just as it was in the days of Lot—they were eating and drinking, buying and selling, *planting and building* (daytime events), but on the day when Lot went out from Sodom, fire and sulfur rained from heaven and destroyed them all—so will it be on the day when the Son of Man is revealed. (Luke 17:28–30, emphasis added)

THIEF IN THE NIGHT

In 1 Thessalonians 5:2–10, the day of the Lord coming like a thief in the night is a metaphor that the Lord's judgment will arrive unexpectedly, catching the wicked off guard. These verses do not suggest that this prophecy will occur in the absence of sunlight or that it is applicable to the righteous.

For you yourselves are fully aware that the day of the Lord will come like a thief in the night. While people are saying, "There is peace and security," then sudden destruction will come upon them (the wicked) as labor pains come upon a pregnant woman, and they will not escape. But you are not in (spiritual) darkness, brothers (the righteous), for that day to surprise you like a thief. (1 Thess. 5:2–4)

1 Thessalonians 5:4 confirms this understanding, indicating that believers are not in spiritual darkness but are enlightened by the truth of Jesus's Word. This is further supported by the description of Jesus's return in Luke 17:28–35, which includes activities like planting and building, suggesting a normal twenty-four-hour day on earth. Therefore, the thief in the night prophecy is not associated with an absence of sunlight.

Luke 17:26–30, drawing parallels to the days of Noah and Lot, supports the interpretation that the righteous will be physically separated, that is raptured, before that day of the Lord. The wicked will fail to recognize the signs of the approaching judgment due to the strong delusion in 2 Thessalonians 2:9–11. The rapture of the church, described in 1 Thessalonians 4:17–18, occurs before the wicked are caught off guard in 1 Thessalonians 5:2–10.

Therefore, the phrase "thief in the night" in 1 Thessalonians 5:2–4 cannot be applied to the midpoint with Jesus's return and the start of the fifth opened seal, when Jacob's trouble and the great tribulation begin. At this midpoint, when Gog and the ten kings are attacking Israel, there is no sense of the 1 Thessalonians 5:3 described "peace and security."

During the events described in the sixth seal (Isa. 2:18–19; Matt. 24:29; Rev. 6:12), the wicked will throw away their idols, expecting physical death though it does not come (Rev. 6:13–17). The next event, seventh opened seal, is derived a normal day, which will give the wicked a false sense of peace and security with the impending day of the Lord in Revelation 8:7. The brothers (righteous), who are not in spiritual darkness, would recognize that their rapture is imminent (1 Thess. 5:4), as in the days of Lot and Noah, and would be rejoicing.

CONCLUSION

This chapter has addressed seven of the prewrath chronological problems and proposed the beyond prewrath solution.

The first six reasons highlight issues with interpreting the sequence of events in Revelation chapters 6 to 8 chronologically. This analysis revealed that the rejoicing of the multitude in heaven described in Revelation 7:9–17 as an immediate consequence of the interpreted earthly rapture depicted in Revelation 8:5 theophany, associated with the opening of the seventh seal. Additionally, the arrival of the 144,000 from the twelve Hebrew tribes (Rev. 7:1–8) appears to coincide with the start of their mission on earth to witness to those who are left behind, likely focused on those who are Jewish.

The seventh reason involves the interpretation of Matthew 24:27, 29, and 30–31 as three distinct and separate chronological events, corresponding to the fifth, sixth, and seventh opened seals, respectively. This interpretation concurs with the understanding established in chapter 1, which identified the coming of Jesus in verse 27 at the midpoint and with the later elect rapture in verses 30–31 with Jesus continued earthly presence. Chronologically separating these verses is verse 29, which parallels the darkness and earthquake depicted in Revelation 6:12 in the sixth opened seal.

Chapter 7

Ezekiel 38–39 Depict Different Battles

PURPOSE

While many scholars interpret Ezekiel 38 and 39 as depicting the same battle called Armageddon, this author holds a differing view. According to this perspective, the battle depicted in Ezekiel 38 occurs when Gog attacks, which aligns with the associated abomination of desolation at the midpoint (Dan. 9:27; Matt. 24:15). Ezekiel 39, however, is proposed to portray two subsequent battles: the Jehoshaphat battle, followed shortly thereafter by the Armageddon battle. Figure 14 provides a visual representation of these distinct battles, followed by a detailed discussion of the Scriptures row by row.

FIGURE 14: EZEKIEL 38–39 DEPICT DIFFERENT BATTLES

When	Ezekiel	Zechariah 14 / Revelation	Acts 2	Matthew 24
Midpoint first battle	Gog attacks from north (38:1–6)	Fly from Satan (Rev. 12:14)		Flee Satan's abomination (vv. 15–16)
	Earthquake (38:19–20)	Earthquake (Zech. 14:5, 10)		
Much later two battles (in sixth trumpet and seventh bowl)	Gog attacks from north (39:1–2)			
	Birds of prey (represents two battles) (39:4, 17–20)	Two hundred million in Jehoshaphat (Rev. 9:16) and Armageddon (Rev. 16:16; 19:11–21)		
	Weapons for fuel (39:9–10)			
	Pour out His Spirit (39:29)		Shall be saved (v. 21)	

FIRST ROW – GOG ATTACKS, ISRAELITES FLEE

In Ezekiel 38:1–6 (first row) and 39:1–2 (third row), both passages depict Gog launching an attack from the north. This duplication in Scripture raises the question of why this attack is described twice. The repetition suggests that these are indeed two distinct attacks. During the first assault, it appears that the Antichrist and the coalition of ten kings do not achieve complete success. This aligns with the imagery presented in Zechariah 14:2, where it states, "The city will be taken … and half of the city shall go out into exile," followed by verse 3, which describes the LORD intervening to fight against those nations. The initial attack by Gog is proposed to take place at the midpoint of the seventieth week, as discussed in chapter 2.

Indeed, the directive for the Israelites to flee is found in the Old Testament passage of Zechariah 14:5, mirroring the New Testament passages in Matthew 24:15–16 and Revelation 12:14. This parallel underscore the continuity between Old Testament prophecy and New Testament revelation regarding the events surrounding the assault and the ensuing response of God in a day of the Lord.

SECOND ROW – GREAT EARTHQUAKE

The second row introduces a unique element: Ezekiel 38:19–20 describes a great earthquake, which is not mentioned chapter 39. This earthquake is proposed to occur chronologically parallel to the events described in Zechariah 14:4 and 10 at the midpoint. In Zechariah 14:10, this earthquake is said to reshape the landscape around Jerusalem, creating a vast plain while leaving the elevation of Jerusalem (city of David and the temple mount) itself unchanged. The epicenter of this great earthquake is located in the land of Israel, as indicated in Ezekiel 38:19–20. The potential damage to airport runways would significantly impede the Israel Defense Force's ability to respond effectively to Gog's attack from their distant undisturbed air bases.

When the Lord responds with a "day of the Lord" in Zechariah 14:1, 3, the attacking force will suffer casualties through fratricide (v. 12), symbolized by brother turning against brother (Ezek. 38:21–23). Additionally, deaths will occur as a result of the Lord's judgment, which includes fire, sulfur, and hailstones (Ezek. 38:22).

For in my jealousy and in my blazing wrath I declare, On that day there shall be a great earthquake in the land of Israel. The fish of the sea and the birds of the heavens and the beasts of the field and all creeping things that creep on the ground, and all the people who are on the face of the earth, shall quake at my presence. And the mountains shall be thrown down, and the cliffs shall fall, and every wall shall tumble to the ground. (Ezek. 38:19–20)

The whole land shall be turned into a plain from Geba to Rimmon south of Jerusalem. But *Jerusalem shall remain aloft* on its site from the Gate of Benjamin to the place of the former gate, to the Corner Gate, and from the Tower of Hananel to the king's winepresses. (Zech. 14:10, emphasis added)

ISRAEL – A LAND OF UNWALLED VILLAGES

Ezekiel 38:11 mentions Gog's intention to go up against the land of unwalled villages. Presently, in East Jerusalem, there are approximately two and a half miles of concrete walls separating it from the Palestinian West Bank, with a height of about thirty-nine feet, for security purposes. However, during the millennial reign of Jesus, there will be peace, except for a little while near the end, rendering such walls unnecessary.

This raises the question of how Ezekiel 38's reference to unwalled villages can be interpreted as occurring during the seventieth week when there is no peace. The apparent explanation lies in Ezekiel 38, verses 19–20, which describes a great earthquake that will cause the walls in Israel to collapse just before the Lord defends Israel from Gog's attack in verses 21–23. Figures 1 and 2 provide support for an earthquake, aligning with Zechariah 14:5, which mentions fleeing to the valley of the mountains due to an earthquake.

Matthew 24:15–16 further supports this timeline, referring to the abomination of desolation standing in the holy place, which is timestamped to the midpoint according to Daniel 9:27. This sequence of events suggests that the reference to unwalled villages in Ezekiel 38 occurs after the earthquake and during the tumultuous period starting at the midpoint.

THIRD ROW – EZEKIEL 39 GOG ATTACKS AGAIN

Ezekiel 39:1–2 depicts Gog launching a second attack from the north. This second assault bolsters the interpretation that his first attack, as described in Ezekiel 38:1–6, was not entirely successful. Hence, it seems reasonable to assume that some time would be required for Gog to regroup his military forces before launching a second attack.

Ezekiel 39:1–5 says this battle is for Gog, deduced to be the second battle called Jehoshaphat. The battle verses 17–20 must be deduced be the later third battle called Armageddon, which is mainly for the kings from the east (Rev. 16:16, 19:11–21, 20:1–3). The third battle is when the beast, false prophet, and Satan are captured.

Furthermore, the Scriptural proximity of the last two eschatological battles, Jehoshaphat and Armageddon, supports the notion of them occurring close to each other chronologically. Chapter 10 of *Jesus's Return Based on the Feasts of the Lord* suggests that the Jehoshaphat battle occurs relatively close before the end of the seventieth week. Armageddon, on the other hand, is associated with the seventh poured bowl (Rev. 19:11–20:3), likely taking place on Day 1,290. The duration of the seven poured bowls is thirty days, derived from passages such as Daniel 9:24–25, 12:11–12 (1,260 days versus 1,290 days) and Revelation 12:14 (three and a half years). Robert Van Kampen's work in *The Sign of Christ's Coming and the End of the Age* supports this understanding.[1]

FOURTH ROW – BIRDS OF PREY

Ezekiel 39 seems to delineate two distinct battles occurring close to each other chronologically, supported by additional lines of reasoning. Firstly, the mention of birds of prey, which would consume human flesh and blood, appears twice: in verse 5 and again in verses 17–21. Interestingly, there is no reference to birds in Ezekiel 38. The proximity of these references within Ezekiel 39, albeit only a few verses apart, suggests the aftermath of two separate battles occurring closely in time. These battles are inferred to be the outcome of the remaining two battles known as Jehoshaphat and Armageddon.

---

1   Robert Van Kampen, *The Sign of Christ's Coming and the End of the Age* (Wheaton, IL: Crossway Books, 1992), 365–368.

The absence of birds in the earlier Ezekiel 38 Jerusalem battle could be attributed to two factors. Firstly, the scale of death in the Jerusalem battle may not be as extensive as in the Jehoshaphat battle, which involves a two-hundred-million-strong army (Rev. 9:16). Secondly, year-round flowing water starting at the midpoint and later poluted water elsewhere on the earth will slowly over about three years bring birds to Israel's living water.

GARDEN OF EDEN

Israel's eschatological agricultural enhancement will occur three times, ultimately leading to the creation of a garden of Eden-like environment. Each enhancement corresponds to one of the three battles of Jesus before the commencement of the millennium.

1) First Agricultural Improvement – Midpoint with the Jerusalem Battle: This takes place at the midpoint with the Jerusalem battle. Later Joel 2:3 Eden prophecy is fulled in the fifth blown trumpet. This transformation involves three main events:

   a. pH Raised: The hills surrounding Jerusalem, typically with a relatively low soil pH due to their steep terrain, will have their pH raised by adding lime derived from pulverized human bones of the battlefield. This process sweetens the soil, making it conducive to healthier vegetation growth. It can take a year or so for the soil pH to be fully sweetened.

   b. Blood Meal: There will also be blood from fratricide (Ezek. 38:21–23).

   c. Terrain Slope Changes: Upon Jesus's return, the mountainous terrain surrounding Jerusalem will be immediately transformed from an earthquake to a gradual downward slope toward the eastern and western seas, as Ezekiel 47:1–6 and Zechariah 14:10 prophecy.

   d. Year-Round Water Source: Israel will have two year-round flowing rivers, east and west, from Jerusalem, prophesied in Isaiah 33:21 and Zechariah 14:8. During the millennium reign of Jesus the river only flows east to the Dead Sea (Zech. 47:3), indicating the westward river dried up at some point prior to the start of the millennium.

2) Second Agricultural Improvement – Jehoshaphat Battle: The second enhancement occurs following the Jehoshaphat battle, where an attacking force of two hundred million is involved (Rev. 9:16). The aftermath of this battle, depicted in Revelation 14:20, involves a significant amount of blood, much of which is consumed by birds of prey (Ezek. 39:4–5, 17–26). The blood and bird droppings serve as organic fertilizer enriched with nitrogen, phosphorus, and potassium, promoting healthier soil.

3) Third Agricultural Improvement – Armageddon Battle: The third enhancement results from the attacking force of the kings from the East and their defeat in the Armageddon battle (Rev. 19:11 – 20:3; cf. 16:12–16). The blood spilled during this battle further enriches the soil, contributing to the organic fertilizer present in the millennium.

GARDEN OF EDEN – IN THE MILLENNIUM

The start of the millennium marks the culmination of all eschatological soil enrichments, terrain improvements, seeds provided from bird droppings, and year-round flowing water transformations in Israel, ultimately rendering it akin to a garden of Eden as described in Ezekiel 36:35. Israel historically is characterized as wilderness in Scripture. The transformation during the millennium will be profound.

FIFTH ROW – CLEANSE THE LAND

In Ezekiel 39:9–10, it says that the fuel from the battles will be utilized for seven years. Diesel is identified as the primary military fuel source, known for its long shelf life, particularly if used solely for fires rather than transportation purposes. Sparks generated from negative and positive battery wires could serve to ignite this fuel source. Given that the Armageddon battle occurs during the pouring out of the seventh bowl, there is no opportunity for Israel to commence collecting weapons for fuel until the beginning of the millennium. This rationale similarly applies to the cleansing of the land of Israel described in verses 11–16.

SIXTH ROW – POURS OUT HIS SPIRIT

Ezekiel 39:29 has the Lord pouring out his spirit on the Jewish people. Pouring out the Lord's spirit is the same thought as the Jewish people calling on the name of the Lord in Acts 2:17–21, which occurs before "the great and magnificent day" deduced to be the Jehoshaphat battle.

CONCLUSION

Ezekiel 38 depicts when Gog and his coalition first attack Israel, known as the Jerusalem battle. Despite Gog's initial success described in Zechariah 14:2, God intervenes to defend Israel (Ezek. 38:21–23). This is expected to slow down the start of the great tribulation, though not stop it (Rev. 12:13–17). This later leads to Gog's subsequent second attack in Ezekiel 39:1–2.

Ezekiel 39 portrays two later battles, deduced to be the Jehoshaphat and Armageddon battles. The first occurs in the sixth blown trumpet when Gog attacks again, while the second is in the seventh poured bowl when the kings from the east attack. These battles, occurring about thirty days apart, are detailed in the same chapter, with the beast, false prophet, and Satan being captured in the third battle.

Acts 2:17–21 is interpreted as applicable to the Jewish people receiving God's spiritual salvation the day before "the great and magnificent day" (Jehoshaphat battle). Later, in the seventh blown trumpet, they are raptured, as depicted with the second great dispensational theophany of Revelation 11:19.

Chapter 8

Israelites: Exile, Exodus, and Return

PURPOSE – THREE SEGMENTED ISRAEL EVENTS

The timeline of the Jewish people in the second half of the seventieth week is delineated into three distinct chronological segments.

First segment: At the midpoint of the seventieth week, many Jewish people must undergo exile from Israel into the surrounding countries. This marks the onset of Jacob's trouble and the great tribulation depicted in the fifth seal, coinciding with the attack of Gog and the ten-king coalition.

Second segment: Those in captivity in Egypt and along the Euphrates River begin their journey to Mt. Sinai. This exodus commences as the tribulation ends with the sixth opened seal and nears completion shortly after the first blown trumpet. Those from Egypt will traverse mostly dry land across the Red Sea, mirroring Israel's first exodus.

Third segment: Jesus engages in battle alone in Bozrah and Edom before making his way to Jerusalem for the Jehoshaphat battle, occurring during the sixth blown trumpet. The Jewish people from Mt. Sinai follow closely behind, likely arriving in Jerusalem shortly after the battle. Those Jewish people elsewhere on earth appear to undergo a horizontal rapture to Jerusalem for the béma judgment when their decreed last prophetic week is complete.

FIRST SEGMENT: ISRAEL GOES INTO EXILE

At the midpoint of the seventieth week, Gog's attack on Israel initiates Jacob's trouble, leading to many in Israel being taken into exile or killed (Zech. 13:8–9). While some remain in Jerusalem, the remnant fleeing to the east are promised nourishment and protection for 1,260 days. This period of Jacob's trouble presents an opportunity for the *sheep* to show kindness to Jesus's brothers (righteous), as Jesus's prophecy in Matthew 25:35–36. If so, then they will inherit the millennium kingdom where they will be reigned over. These works-based acts of kindness are likely during the great tribulation, indicated especially by verse 36 to visit those in prison. The first segment concludes with the opening of the sixth seal.

SECOND SEGMENT: EXODUS TO MT. SINAI

Matthew 24:29 and Revelation 6:12 prophesy the end of the great tribulation with the opening of the sixth seal, marked by a world-wide great earthquake and darkness. Jeremiah 30:8 describes this as the end of the Jewish persecution. This sets the stage for the second segment of the exodus to Mt. Sinai.

Separately, Isaiah 11 speaks of a later final "second" exodus before the end of Jesus millennium reign.

> And it shall come to pass in that day, declares the Lord of hosts, that I will break his yoke from off your neck, and I will burst your bonds, and foreigners shall no more make a servant of him. (Jer. 30:8)

The liberation of the Jewish people from exile, and the church from imprisoned persecution, may mirror biblical accounts of the apostles being set free from imprisonment, such as Peter (Acts 12:5–17) and Paul (Acts 16:22–30). This is an end to world-wide persecution against faith in Jesus.

The Jewish people's exodus from exile to Mt. Sinai parallels their historical exodus from Egypt, featuring similar elements:

1) The Lord's intervention symbolized by riding on a swift cloud.
2) Crossing of the dry waterbed of the Red Sea, reminiscent of the miraculous event in Exodus.
3) Journey to Mt. Sinai, reminiscent of the book of Exodus.

SECOND SEGMENT, ELEMENT 1: LORD ON A CLOUD

Israel's first exodus from Egypt was with the LORD leading them in a pillar of cloud in Exodus 13:17–22. In a similar way eschatological Isaiah 19:1 has them relenting and the LORD traveling on a swift cloud. Numbers 24:8 goes further to describe judgment of his adversaries. Hosea 11:10–11 has the LORD roaring like a lion with his children coming from Egypt and Assyria. This is in contrast to Jesus's first advent when he came as the Lamb of God to be sacrificed as an atonement for our sins (1 John 2:2). Hosea 2:15 has its first of two prophecies fulfilled when Jesus returned to Israel in Matthew 2:15, after the death of Herod.

They shall go after the LORD;
  he will roar like a lion;
when he roars,
  his children shall come trembling
from the west;
  they shall come trembling like birds from Egypt,
and like doves from the land of Assyria.
(Hosea 11:10–11a)

And the LORD went before them by day in a pillar of cloud to lead them along the way, and by night in a pillar of fire to give them light, that they might travel by day and by night. The pillar of cloud by day and the pillar of fire by night did not depart from before the people. (Ex. 13:21–22)

An oracle concerning Egypt.

Behold, the LORD is riding on a swift cloud
  and comes to Egypt;
and the idols of Egypt will tremble at his presence,
  and the heart of the Egyptians will melt within them.
(Isa. 19:1)

SECOND SEGMENT, ELEMENT 2: RED SEA

In the first exodus, the Israelites experienced a miraculous crossing of the Red Sea, where the waters parted to allow them safe passage. Similarly, prophetic passages anticipate a future divine intervention to facilitate the remnant of Israel's journey to safety amidst global upheaval.

This intervention begins with the end of the great tribulation in Matthew 24:29. This is when the LORD recovers his remnant (cf. Ex. 14), in reference to Egypt and other nearby countries.

SECOND SEGMENT, ELEMENT 3: TO MT. SINAI

The second segment of the Israelite's journey involves their exodus from Egypt to Mt. Sinai, mirroring their historic journey following the first Passover. Just as they were led by God from bondage to freedom in the wilderness, a remnant will embark on a similar journey of deliverance during the end-times.

- Historical Exodus:

    1. Starting Point: The first exodus commenced on Nisan 15 (Num. 33:3), the day after the Passover, when the Israelites departed from Egypt.

    2. Ending Point: The journey concluded on the third new moon, Sivan 1 (Ex. 19:1), when they arrived at the wilderness of Sinai.

    3. Path and Duration: The route and duration of the first exodus, calculated based on the Jewish calendar, provide insights into the expected journey of the remnant of Israel during the eschatological end times. This journey spanned forty-six days, according to starting and ending points above.

- Eschatological Exodus:

    1. Commencement: This eschatological exodus is anticipated to begin following the end of the great tribulation, marked by the opening of the sixth seal. This period of upheaval and turmoil will culminate in the deliverance of God's people from oppression and persecution.

    2. Starting Point: Countries surrounding Israel specified in Ezekiel 30:5–6.

    3. Duration: The duration of the first exodus to reach the safety of the wilderness (several days short of the forty-six days to Mt. Sinai) appears to correspond to the timeframe of the sixth and seventh opened seals when there is no tribulation (figure 13).[1]

---

1 The first exodus of just under forty-six days to arrive at safety across the Red Sea adds support for the eschatological total duration analysis of chapters 3 and 4 from *Beyond Prewrath End-Time Prophecy.*

This allows for a similar path of deliverance for the remnant of Israel.

4. Path: Those returning from Egypt will traverse a path reminiscent of their historic journey, crossing through tumultuous events and obstacles to reach their destination of safety and refuge.

5. Destination: The destination of this exodus is Mt. Sinai, symbolizing a place of encounter with God and covenant renewal, as seen in the historical account.

•   Significance: The repetition of the exodus journey highlights God's faithfulness in delivering His people from bondage and leading them to freedom and covenant relationship. This symbolic journey serves as a testament to God's promises of protection and provision for His Jewish chosen people, even amidst trials and tribulations.

The Israelites' arriving at the wilderness before the first trumpet is blown should allow them enough time to make it into present-day Jordan. We know from Daniel 11:41 that the historical area of Jordan, which encompasses Moab and parts of Edom, "shall be delivered out of his (Antichrist's) hands." Such that, when the trumpet judgments begin, they will have safety. Some persecution is possible in the blown trumpets since the wicked are recognized with idols again in the fifth blown trumpet of Revelation 9:20.

Mt. Sinai, located in Arabia (Gal. 4:25), is their second segment destination. Later, in the sixth blown trumpet, near the end of the seventieth week, they will be commanded to leave Mt. Sinai to avoid Gog's second attack on Babylon (Rev. 18:4). This begins their third travel segment.

Then I heard another voice from heaven saying,

"Come out of her, my people,
  lest you take part in her sins,
lest you share in her plagues."
(Rev. 18:4)

Writhe and groan, O daughter of Zion,
  like a woman in labor,
for now you shall go out from the city
  and dwell in the open country;
  you shall go to Babylon.
There you shall be rescued;
  there the LORD will redeem you
  from the hand of your enemies.
(Micah 4:10)

THIRD SEGMENT: MT. SINAI TO JERUSALEM

The final segment of the Jewish people's journey in the end-times narrative involves their transition from Mt. Sinai to Bozrah, Edom, and eventually Jerusalem.

- Jesus's Role in the Battle: Isaiah 63:1–3 has Jesus as the sole combatant in the battle against Bozrah. This battle represents a decisive victory over evil forces and the restoration of divine justice, followed by the Jehoshaphat battle at Jerusalem.

- Timing of the Battle: The battle at Bozrah and Edom likely occurs during the sixth blown trumpet, preceding or coinciding with the Jehoshaphat battle in Jerusalem. This timing aligns with the progression of end-times events and the fulfillment of biblical prophecy.

- Consequence of the Battle: Malachi 4:2–3 describes the aftermath of the Jehoshaphat battle where Israel treads upon the wicked ashes under their feet. This imagery symbolizes a major step toward complete triumph of righteousness over evil.

- Biblical References: Deuteronomy 33:1–2 and Judges 5:4–5 provide additional scriptural support for the divine intervention at Bozrah, Edom, and Sinai. These passages highlight the presence of God in the midst of battle, emphasizing His authority and power to bring about victory.

- Parallel with Revelation: The imagery of treading in the winepress in Isaiah 63:3 parallels the description of blood trampled outside the city in Revelation 14:20. This suggests a symbolic connection between the cleansing of Jerusalem and the defeat of God's enemies in the next to last final battle. The final cleansing of the land in Israel will begin when Jesus's thousand-year reign begins.

Overall, the journey from Mt. Sinai to Bozrah, Edom, and Jerusalem represents a pivotal phase in the end-times narrative, marked by Jesus's culmination of the second battle called Jehoshaphat.

> Who is this who comes from Edom,
>   in crimsoned garments from Bozrah,
> he who is splendid in his apparel,
>   marching in the greatness of his strength?
> "It is I, speaking in righteousness,
>   mighty to save. (cf. Acts 2:21)"
> Why is your apparel red,
>   and your garments like his who treads in the winepress?
> "I have trodden the winepress alone,
>   and from the peoples no one was with me.
> (Isa. 63:1–3a)

> But for you who fear my name, the sun of righteousness shall rise with healing in its wings. You shall go out leaping like calves from the stall. And you shall tread down the wicked, for they will be ashes under the soles of your feet, on the day when I act, says the LORD of hosts. (Mal. 4:2–3)

> And the winepress was trodden outside the city, and blood flowed from the winepress, as high as a horse's bridle, for 1,600 stadia. (Rev. 14:20)

THIRD SEGMENT: OTHER JEWISH PEOPLE

For Jewish people located far from the region of Israel and Mt. Sinai, the journey to these locations during the tumultuous events of the end-times presents practical challenges and uncertainties. It is unclear whether they will have the opportunity or means to travel to these destinations within the limited timeframe between the cessation of great tribulation and the onset of the trumpet judgments.

- Challenges of Travel: The period of relative calm during the sixth and seventh opened seals, estimated to last almost forty-six days (historic exodus of Nisan 15 to Sivan 1), may not provide enough time for Jewish people in distant locations to undertake the journey to Mt. Sinai. Additionally, the impending trumpet judgments, with their accompanying persecution and idolatry, could deter or impede travel efforts.

- Potential Stay in Place: It is possible that Jewish people in distant locations may opt to remain where they are, rather than attempting to journey to Mt. Sinai. The uncertain and perilous conditions of the end-times may discourage movement, leading individuals and communities to prioritize safety and stability.

- Second Rapture and Relocation: The second rapture represented in Revelation 11:19 theophany marks the end of the seventieth week of Daniel and the gathering of all spiritually saved Jewish people and anyone else calling on the name of the Lord. While these individuals may not be taken to heaven immediately, they could be relocated to Jerusalem for the judgment at the béma (Rev. 11:18), similar to the apostle Philip's rapture to another place on earth as in Acts 8:26–40. This seems to be a reflection of Isaiah 27:13, "And in that day a great trumpet will be blown, and those who were lost … will come and worship the LORD on the holy mountain at Jerusalem." That great trumpet seems to be the seventh and last blown trumpet.

- Post Béma Events: Following the béma judgment, the wedding and marriage supper of the Lamb occur (Rev. 19:9–10). The subsequent cohabitation of the bride and bridegroom takes place on earth during Jesus's thousand-year reign, symbolized with Jesus in Mt. Zion (Jerusalem). This newlywed location interpretation, where the bride lived previously (on earth), is supported by historical context, such as the portrayal of Jewish wedding customs in the Catholic Bible's Tobit 7:19 to 8:1.

- New earth and heaven: The eventual establishment of Jesus's new earth and new heaven in Revelation 21, offers hope for a permanent and blessed dwelling place for the bride and groom, symbolizing the fulfillment of God's promises for His people without death and sin.

In summary, the challenges and uncertainties faced by the Jewish people in distant locations during the end-times highlight the complexities of their journey and the need for reliance on divine guidance and providence.

CONCLUSION

The journey of the Jewish people during the second half of the seventieth week of Daniel is characterized by three distinct segmented events, each marked by significant developments and challenges:

1) First Segment - Forced Captivity: This period is initiated by the abomination of desolation at the midpoint of the seventieth week. Many Jewish people are subjected to forced captivity in nearby foreign countries, beginning a time of tribulation known as Jacob's trouble. The onset of this segment coincides with the opening of the fifth seal, signaling a time of persecution and distress, though a remnant will flee for three and half years of protection and nourishment.

2) Second Segment - Exodus from Exile to Mt. Sinai: With the temporary cessation of worldwide persecution and the start of the sixth opened seal, the Jewish people begin their exodus from exile to Mt. Sinai. This journey mirrors the biblical exodus from Egypt with the end of the great tribulation and the beginning of a short period of relative calm. The route to Mt. Sinai is undertaken as a symbolic pilgrimage, marked by divine guidance and protection.

3) Third Segment - Return to Jerusalem: As the sixth trumpet is sounded, signifying the commencement of significant eschatological events, the Jewish people make their way back to Jerusalem. This return coincides with their spiritual salvation, as described in Acts 2:21. The end of the seventieth week marks their rapture, likely to Jerusalem for the judgment at the béma. This rapture event, occurring at the conclusion of the seventy weeks decreed for the Jewish people, symbolizes the fulfillment of the prophecy in Daniel 9:24–25.

In summary, the segmented timeline of the Jewish people during the second half of the seventieth week underscores the challenges, trials, and ultimate redemption woven into their end-times narrative. From forced captivity to spiritual salvation and rapture, their journey reflects the unfolding of God's sovereign plan for the Jewish people.

Chapter 9

Seals and Trumpets Do Not Overlap

PURPOSE

The purpose of this chapter is to demonstrate that the first two chronological sets of septets in the book of Revelation—the seven opened seals and seven blown trumpets—do not overlap. The aim is to show a clear and non-overlapping sequential framework where each septet follows in succession without overlapping with the others. There are other authors who demonstrate that the last two sets of septets, seven blown trumpets, and seven poured bowls, do not chronologically overlap.[1]

TYPES OF SEQUENTIAL FRAMEWORK

Three types of sequential septet frameworks proposed by scholars are outlined. This author supports the third framework.

1) Full Overlapping: Each of the seven events within each of the three sets of septets all overlap and, therefore, occur simultaneously.

2) Partial Overlapping: The seventh opened seal overlaps all of the seven blown trumpets, and the seventh blown trumpet overlaps all seven poured bowls.

3) No Overlapping: Beyond prewrath exegesis posits this framework, which is none of the three septets overlap.

NO OVERLAPPING FRAMEWORK

The no overlapping framework is supported by the beyond prewrath exegesis, particularly in Revelation 8:5 and 8:7. This interpretation suggests that the elect rapture occurs in the seventh opened seal before the associated day of the Lord, represented by the first blown trumpet. This is in line with Jesus's prophecy in Luke 17:22–30, where the righteous are separated from physical harm on the same day before the judgment against the wicked.

---

1   Dr. Alan Kurschner audio recording, Eschatos Ministries, accessed August 11, 2024, http://www.alankurschner.com/2015/06/04/.

In chapter 5, the third prewrath problem was analyzed, offering an exegesis that Revelation 8:5 symbolizes the first great dispensational theophany, indicative of a day of Christ (rapture of the elect). Furthermore, the fourth prewrath problem presented an exegesis suggesting that Revelation 8:7, depicting fire and death, mirrors the scenario described in Luke 17:28–30, where fire and sulfur are used against the wicked reminiscent of the judgment upon Sodom and Gomorrah (Gen. 19:1–29).

CONCLUSION

The chapter concludes by affirming that according to the beyond prewrath exegesis, the sequential seven opened seals and the seven blown trumpets do not overlap. The elect rapture (a day of Christ) must occur before though on the same day "day of the Lord," as Jesus prophesized with Lot and Noah. The beyond prewrath exegesis has the first event (day of Christ) in the seventh opened seal of Revelation 8:5 and the same day second event in the first blown trumpet (day of the Lord) in verse 7. This then demands a non-overlapping sequence interpretation of the seven sequential opened seals and seven sequential blown trumpets..

Chapter 10

Antichrist and the Restrainer

PURPOSE

To explore the different beings of the unholy trinity and the concept of the restrainer. First, to differentiate this satanic trinity, it is proposed that the Antichrist is a composite being consisting of two entities: a physical being (a man) who becomes indwelt by Satan (a spiritual being) after being cast from heaven to earth. This Antichrist will exist on earth only until the conclusion of the battle of Armageddon, when the man of lawlessness (a beast) is captured, as described in Revelation 19:19–20, along with Satan in Revelation 20:1–3. The third being in this satanic trinity is the false prophet. The following discussion will delve further into these satanic figures.

1) Little horn (Dan. 7:8)
2) Prince (Dan. 9:26)
3) Gog (Ezek. 38:2–3, 14–16; 39:1–16; Rev. 20:8)
4) Man of lawlessness, son of destruction (2 Thess. 2:3)
5) Antichrist (1 John 2:18)
6) Antichrist (1 John 2:22)
7) Dragon, serpent, devil, Satan (Rev. 12, 20)
8) Beast of the sea (Rev. 13:1)
9) Beast of the earth (Rev. 13:11)
10) Beast, dragon and false prophet (Rev. 16:13)
11) Beast and false prophet (Rev. 19:20)
12) Dragon, serpent, devil, Satan (Rev. 20:1–3)

The eschatological restrainer mentioned in 2 Thessalonians 2:7 is proposed to be the archangel, Michael. He is restraining Satan and his angels in heaven until it is time for their restraints to be released. Then a heavenly battle ensues, and they are thrown from heaven to earth at the midpoint to fulfill the timing of prophecy.

FIGURE 15: SATAN THROWN OUT OF HEAVEN

Daniel 9	Matthew 24	2 Thessalonians 2 / Revelation 12
		Satan thrown out of heaven. His time is short. (Rev. 12:7–12)
Abomination of desolation at midpoint (v. 27)	Abomination of desolation (v. 15)	Takes his seat in the temple (2 Thess. 2:4)
	Israel told to flee (vv. 16–20)	Woman (Israel) pursued by the dragon (Rev. 12:13–16)
	Great tribulation of the elect (vv. 21–22)	Dragon makes war on the woman's offspring (church) (Rev. 12:17)

TWO TYPES OF ANTICHRISTS

There are two types of antichrists: general (antichrist) and specific (Antichrist). Since many antichrists have existed throughout history, we must then distinguish them from the eschatological Antichrist. Many scholars say the Antichrist comes into existence with the prophet Daniel's little horn, which is just before the start of the seventieth week of Daniel. I disagree.

Beyond prewrath has the little horn as a general antichrist, though not the specific Antichrist until Satan indwells within him at the midpoint of the seventieth week. As a man, we would anticipate this man of lawlessness would have been born on the earth.

> Little children, it is the last hour; and as you have heard that the *Antichrist* (specific) is coming (eschatological), even now *many antichrists* (general) have come, by which we know that it is the last hour. (1 John 2:18 NKJV, emphasis added)

> Who is a liar but he who denies that Jesus is the Christ? He is antichrist who denies the Father and the Son. (general). (1 John 2:22 NKJV)

LITTLE HORN

The little horn is referenced in Daniel 7:8. As a horn, Daniel 7:24 considers him to have a kingdom. Later in Daniel 9:27 he makes the covenant with many strong, which starts the prophetic seventieth week of Daniel. This author interprets that the little horn may give away his kingdom during or before the first opened seal (though still having secretive control) in order to mitigate himself from being revealed until the midpoint with the abomination of desolation. Those who have wisdom will be able to identify the beast before the midpoint using the number of the man 666 (Rev. 13:18).

> And the *people* (ten horns representing the ten kings) of the *prince* (little horn, Dan. 7:8) who is to come shall destroy the city and the sanctuary. Its end shall come with a flood, and to the end there shall be war. (Dan. 9:26b, emphasis added)

GOG AND THE PRINCE

Gog, the chief prince of Meshech and Tubal, attacks Israel in Ezekiel 38 and 39 from the north. This prince is considered the same prince who adds support to the signed covenant or treaty in Daniel 9:27 at the start of the seventieth week, though forty-two months later breaks it by attacking and abomination of desolation. Ezekiel 38:5 has him with a coalition of other armies, which this author considers representative of the ten horns (kings) of Revelation 17:12–15.

MAN OF LAWLESSNESS IS A BEAST

Judas Iscariot was the first person called the son of destruction in John 17:12. He betrayed Jesus and later killed himself. There is a future eschatological son of destruction in 2 Thessalonians 2:3. The title is used interchangeable with the man of lawlessness. Judas was a man born on earth, just as we would expect the eschatological man of lawlessness to be.

Both of these men (beasts) seem to be representative of Revelation 17:11, "As for the beast that was and is not (Judas Iscariot), it is an eighth (eschatological man of lawlessness) but it belongs to the seven, and it goes to destruction." The seven is in reference to seven empire heads, that is the first four are Egyptian, Assyrian, Babylonian, and Medo-Persian. Just as Satan (a spirit being) indwelt within Judas (a man), there is a precedence for Satan to again indwell within this eschatological beast (man) with the number 666. This is expected to occur at the midpoint when Satan is thrown out of heaven in Revelation 12, which starts the great tribulation. The woman, Israel remnant, is protected and nourished for three and a half years in verse 14. This is where a time is one year, times is two years, and half a time is half a year. She is proposed to be raptured the last day of this protection (Day 1,260), thus also fulfilling to the day the Daniel 9:24–25 prophecy of seventy weeks decreed for the Jewish people.

Therefore, this beast is the man of lawlessness. He is initially only an antichrist. It is only when Satan is thrown from heaven at the midpoint and indwells within this man at the midpoint that he becomes the Antichrist.

> Then after he had taken the morsel, Satan entered into him (Judas). Jesus said to him, "What you are going to do, do quickly." (John 13:27)

> While I was with them, I kept them in your name, which you have given me. I have guarded them, and not one of them has been lost except the son of destruction (Judas), that the Scripture might be fulfilled. (John 17:12)

SATAN AND THE BEAST ARE DIFFERENT BEINGS

Satan in Revelation 12 is thrown from heaven to earth. The beast of Revelation 17:8 comes from the bottomless pit to earth. Since each arrive to earth from a different location, they should be considered different beings.

> But he was defeated, and there was no longer any place for them in heaven. And the great dragon was thrown down, that ancient serpent, who is called the devil and Satan, the deceiver of the whole world—he was thrown down to the earth, and his angels were thrown down with him. (Rev. 12:8–9)

> The beast that you saw was, and is not, and is about to rise from the bottomless pit and go to destruction. (Rev. 17:8a)

BEAST OF THE SEA IS THE ANTICHRIST

Revelation 12 and 17:8 analysis previously supported the beast as a man. Previously also, it was supported that Satan, a spirit being, will enter the man of lawlessness, also called the son of destruction, when he is thrown from heaven. This indwelling occurred before when Satan entered Judas Iscariot in John 13:27, also called a son of destruction. The beast of the sea (Rev. 13:1) will be shown to represent this plural being called the Antichrist.

Scripture supports the "sea" as prophetically representative of the Gentiles. Daniel 7 and Revelation 13 support this theme of the beast coming up out of the Gentile "sea."

- Isaiah 60 is about the future glory of Israel during the millennium when the sea (Gentile wealth) will come to Israel (Jewish people).
- Revelation 17:15b: The sea, a body of water, symbolizes "peoples and multitudes and nations and tongues."

> because the abundance of the sea (Gentile nation) shall be turned to you,
>> the wealth of the nations shall come to you (Israel).
> (Isa. 60:5b)

Therefore, the Revelation 13:1 beast (man) is prophetically rising out of the Gentile nation and is not from the Jewish tribes. Isaiah 27:1a describes the punishment of the serpent, which reflects the capture and binding of Satan on a long chain as depicted in Revelation 20:1–3. Isaiah 27:1b "dragon that is in the sea" being slain must refer to the beast—a physical entity—killed in Revelation 19:19–20, which Satan, a spiritual being, had indwelt. This slaying marks the end of the plural entity known as the Antichrist.

> In that day (Armageddon battle) the LORD with his hard and great and strong sword (cf. Rev. 19:15) will punish Leviathan the fleeing serpent, Leviathan the twisting serpent, and he will slay *the dragon that is in the sea.* (Isa. 27:1, emphasis added)

> And they worshiped the *dragon* (a spirit being), for he had given his authority to the *beast* (a physical man), and they worshiped the beast, saying, "Who is like the beast, and who can fight against it?" (Rev. 13:4, emphasis added)

> It exercises all the authority of the first beast (Scripture was explicit to say the first beast and not just a beast as in verse 4) in its presence, and makes the earth and its inhabitants worship the first beast, whose mortal wound was healed. (Rev. 13:12)

The Revelation 13:1 *beast* (man) that rises out the sea and the Revelation 12:3 *great red dragon* (Satan) both are described as having ten horns and seven heads. They both have the exact same attributes, indicating a plural entity. How is it possible that two can be one? The reason is that the beast (man) is physical, though Satan is spiritual. This points us to Satan indwelling with the man. This plural entity is called the unique eschatological Antichrist.

> As for the ten horns, out of this kingdom ten kings (horn=king) shall arise, and another shall arise after them. (Dan. 7:24a)

> And another sign appeared in heaven: behold, a great red dragon (represents Satan), with *seven heads and ten horns, and on his heads seven diadems.* (Rev. 12:3, emphasis added)

> And I saw a beast (man of lawlessness) rising out of the sea, with *ten horns and seven heads, with ten diadems* on its horns and blasphemous names on its heads. (Rev. 13:1, emphasis added)

BEAST OF THE EARTH IS THE FALSE PROPHET

The beast of the earth is the false prophet as described by its attributes of Revelation 13. Most, if not all, scholars support this understanding.

> Verse 11: Then I saw another beast rising out of the earth (false prophet). It had two horns like a lamb, and it spoke like a dragon.

> Verse 13: Performs great signs.

> Verse 14: Deceives those on the earth.

> Verse 15: It was allowed to give breath to the image of the beast.

BEAST OF REVELATION 16 AND 19

The logistics of troops moving to the battlefield from the east in Revelation 16 in the sixth bowl seems to match the later battle in Revelation 19:11–21.

> The sixth angel poured out his bowl on the great river Euphrates, and its water was dried up, to prepare the way for the kings from the east. (Rev. 16:12)

> Then I saw heaven opened, and behold, a white horse! The one sitting on it is called Faithful and True, and in righteousness he judges and makes war. His eyes are like a flame of fire, and on his head are many diadems, and he has a name written that no one knows but himself. (Rev. 19:11–12)

Revelation 16:13 and 19:20 to 20:2 each identify the same three separate beings: dragon, beast, and false prophet.

> And I saw, coming out of the mouth of the *dragon* (Satan) and out of the mouth of the *beast* (man of lawlessness) and out of the mouth of the false prophet, three unclean spirits like frogs. (Rev. 16:13, emphasis added)

> And the *beast* (man of lawlessness) was captured, and with it the false prophet who in its presence had done the signs by which he deceived those who had received the mark of the beast and those who worshiped its image. These two were thrown alive into the lake of fire that burns with sulfur. (Rev. 19:20, emphasis added)

> And he seized the dragon, that ancient serpent, who is the devil and Satan, and bound him for a thousand years. (Rev. 20:2)

In 2 Thessalonians 2:1–4 the son of destruction was shown to be a man. By deduction the Antichrist is a *beast* (man of lawlessness) indwelt by *Satan* (spirit being). This deduction is supported by the previous paragraphs of analysis.

WHITE HORSE AS A WEDDING GIFT

The white horse should be viewed as a wedding gift. First, Revelation 19:11a describes the horse coming from heaven. Second, at that time, the Father was in heaven, while His Son, Jesus, had been on earth since the midpoint. Given that Jesus's wedding (Rev. 19:7–9) occurred immediately before the appearance of the horse, it can be understood as a wedding gift.

FIGURE 16: UNHOLY TRINITY

Unholy Trinity		
Beast	Satan (Dragon)	False Prophet
Beast (man of lawlessness) with ten horns and seven heads (Rev. 13:1)	Red dragon, a spirit being, with seven heads and ten horns (Rev. 12:3)	Second beast rising out of the earth (Rev. 13:11)
First beast rising from the sea. (Rev. 13:1). Dragon and beast (Rev. 13:4). Satan is proposed to enter the beast (man) at the midpoint to become the Antichrist.		
Mouth of the beast (Rev. 16:13)	Mouth of Satan (Rev. 16:13)	Mouth of the false prophet (Rev. 16:13)
Beast captured (Rev. 19:19)	Satan bound (Rev. 20:1–3)	False prophet captured (Rev. 19:19)

SATAN THROWN OUT OF HEAVEN BY RESTRAINER

Revelation 12:7 identifies that it was the archangel Michael and his angels, who overcame, and threw Satan and his angels (cf. 2 Thess. 2:6) out of heaven to the earth. From this perspective, it seems their restraints were authorized to be released and then the battle in heaven began. Since Michael took the leadership role in the battle, it would seem he would have also taken the previous action to have their restraints unbound, knowing full well that a spiritual battle in heaven would then begin immediately.

Daniel 12:1 says that Michael will arise or "stand up" (NKJV). Many scholars interpret Michael standing up as getting out of the way. But when war breaks out in heaven in Revelation 12, it is Michael who takes the lead to throw Satan and all his angels from heaven to earth. His actions do not give the impression that he is getting out of the way by standing up. An analogy is with Aaron in Exodus 32:1 where he was asked, "Up, make us gods." Then in verses 2–4 Aaron took ungodly leadership to have the golden calf built while Moses was with God on the mountain. To arise or stand up should be considered a metaphor to taking leadership action, whether good or bad (cf. 1 Sam. 9:3). Michael's actions should be considered godly since it is shown he allowed prophecy to be fulfilled (Dan. 9:27; Matt. 24:15; Rev. 12:13–16).

Satan losing the heavenly battle and being thrown to earth is a representation of his parousia where he fell "like lightning from heaven" in Luke 10:18. Satan's parousia can also be found in 2 Thessalonians 2:9, supported in chapter 1 of this book as at the midpoint. The Revelation 12:7–12 spiritual battle verses do not reference Jesus in heaven, so it seems his parousia, from heaven to earth, was earlier to the Mt. of Olives. Both arrive at that same midpoint day.

Therefore, the restrainer is the archangel Michael who restrains Satan until the midpoint when it is time for him to issue the order to remove their restraints and throw Satan and his angels out of heaven to earth. Daniel's (Jewish) "people shall be delivered (Dan. 12:1)," seems representative of the remnant being granted relief (2 Thess. 1:7) from the great tribulation.

SATAN CAPTURED THREE TIMES AND RELEASED TWICE

Satan is captured three times. His first capture date is sometime before his restraints are unbound at the midpoint date; then the heavenly battle occurs with him being thrown to earth (Rev. 12:7–12). His second capture date is in Revelation 20:1–3 as a consequence of the Armageddon battle. Satan's third and final capture date is in Revelation 20:7–10 near the end of Jesus's thousand year reign on earth.

Satan is released twice between his three capture dates. He is first released on earth for about 1,290 days (from Day 1 at the midpoint with the fifth opened seal to the seventh poured bowl on Day 1,290). During these 1,290 days Gog attacks Israel three times (once for each battle), as discussed in chapter 7. Satan is released for a second time after a thousand years, near the end of Jesus's thousand year reign (Rev. 20:7). He will then attack Israel again, with a final Jewish exile and exodus (Isa. 11:11–16; Rev. 20:7–10).

WHEN IS SATAN RESTRAINED?

Nowhere in Scripture does it say, prior to the Revelation 12:7–9 heavenly battle, when Satan and his demonic angels are restrained. The last chronological Satan reference in Scripture was about two thousand years ago when Satan's spirit entered Judas Iscariot and a short time later betrayed Jesus. Perhaps Satan is captured just before the eschatological man of lawlessness is born on earth to prevent the Antichrist from coming into existence before the midpoint? It could be much later, considering the analogy that Satan's spirit did not indwell within Judas Iscariot when he was born, though later on the day when Judas betrayed Jesus. A case can be made that they were restrained just before the start of the seventieth week since Satan is not mentioned in the first half of the seventieth week in Matthew 24:4–15 and Revelation 6:1–8.

CONCLUSION

The midpoint is when Satan and his angels are released from their constraints in heaven, the battle begins in heaven, and then they are thrown from heaven to earth. Revelation 12:7 has Michael taking the leadership role in the heavenly battle; therefore, there is good support that he also took the leadership to have their restraints unbound. Michael standing up in Daniel 12:1 should be considered him taking action to issue the order to release their constraints and not the prevalent view that he is getting out of the way. His release date order seems to be timed with the midpoint to fulfill the midpoint prophecy.

When Satan (a spirit being) arrives on earth, he indwells within the man of lawlessness (a beast). Prior to the midpoint, this beast should be considered an antichrist. At the midpoint they both become the Antichrist.

This perspective is reflective of the two entities of the beast of the sea (Rev. 13:1–10), which is representative of the plural named Antichrist. The first entity is the dragon (spirit) who gave his authority to the beast (man) of Revelation 13:4. That is, Satan gave his authority to the man, whom he indwelt within. The Unholy Trinity of figure 16 shows how this understanding agrees with the book of Revelation 16.

Chapter 11

Endurance and Faith in Jesus

PURPOSE

This chapter explores the two scriptural components necessary to survive the Antichrist's great tribulation and Jacob's trouble: endurance and faith in Jesus, as described in Matthew 13:20–21 and in Revelation 13:10 and 14:12. It emphasizes the dual mandate of both aspects. While many scholars discuss faith in Jesus, they often neglect to address the importance of endurance.

> As for what was sown on rocky ground, this is the one who hears the word and immediately receives it with joy, yet he has no root in himself, but *endures for a while*, and when tribulation or persecution arises on account of the word, immediately he falls away. (Matt. 13:20–21, emphasis added)

> Here is a call for the *endurance* and faith of the saints. (Rev. 13:10b, emphasis added)

> Here is a call for the *endurance of the saints*, those who keep the commandments of God and their faith in Jesus. (Rev. 14:12, emphasis added)

ENDURE AND HAVE FAITH

To physically endure scripturally does not imply that eternal salvation is works-based. Instead, it refers to persevering through the great tribulation when no one can buy or sell without the mark of the beast. Those who take the mark, worship the beast, and worship its image face eternal consequences as outlined in the third angel proclamation. Endurance entails holding onto one's spiritual salvation during a time of extreme persecution. Those who overcome this persecution will retain their eternal salvation and therefore not lose their rewards in heaven. Conversely, those who do not endure physically and apostatize against the Holy Spirit by taking the mark, worshiping the beast, and its image (Rev. 14:9–11) will experience a strong delusion, as described in 2 Thessalonians 2:11, making repentance impossible before their physical death.

THE CHURCH MUST PREPARE TO ENDURE

The eschatological bride of Christ is likened to the ten virgins who must awaken and prepare to endure the coming great tribulation. This preparation begins with an awareness of the prophetic Matthew 24 signs, particularly when Israel signs a treaty with many for seven years (2,520 days). Half of the virgins, as depicted in the eschatological Matthew 25:1–13 parable, will heed the call to prepare. Their endurance will involve readiness to live in a time when Revelation 13:16–17 says that no one can buy or sell without the mark of the beast.

As the great tribulation approaches, with its midpoint (Matt. 24:15) start marked moments before by the three angelic worldwide proclamations (Rev. 14:6–11; cf. Matt. 24:14), global upheaval is anticipated. Therefore, the importance of thorough preparation well in advance of this midpoint cannot be overstated.

> Also it causes all, both small and great, both rich and poor, both free and slave, to be marked on the right hand or the forehead, so that no one can buy or sell unless he has the mark, that is, the name of the beast or the number of its name. (Rev. 13:16–17)

HOW DO WE PREPARE TO ENDURE

First and foremost, preparation involves growing in faith. Romans 10:17 emphasizes that faith comes from hearing the Word of Christ, while Hebrews 11:1 defines faith as "the assurance of things hoped for, the conviction of things not seen." It is imperative, regardless of where we are relative to the coming rapture, to actively apply our faith by boldly witnessing to unbelievers. As the seventieth week commences, our faith must be energized, beyond where we were previously, to both boldly proclaim the Gospel and take physical action to endure the extreme persecution until the time the great tribulation ends, followed shortly by the rescue through a rapture.

In Mark 4:17, it is noted that those who lack a strong foundation in the Word of God will only "endure for a while" when tribulation begins. This echoes the sentiment expressed in Matthew 24:9, particularly evident in the events surrounding the opening of the fourth seal, just before the midpoint, where there is a falling away of the church as described in 2 Thessalonians 2:1–4.

And they have no root in themselves, but endure for a while; then, when tribulation or persecution arises on account of the word, immediately they fall away. (Mark 4:17)

Preparing to endure for the great persecution involves practical actions, such as ensuring our sustenance needs and acquiring necessary medication to survive when buying or selling without the mark of the beast is implemented. This proactive approach is often associated with being a "prepper," someone who strives to live as independently from the worldly system as possible. In Revelation 12:14, even Israel (symbolized as a woman) is provided with nourishment during Jacob's trouble for three and a half years, enabling her to endure. This Israel remnant is the only one promised protection and sustenance during the second half of the seventieth week.

Throughout the Old Testament, we observe examples of preppers who recognized the critical importance of self-sufficiency, understanding that it could mean the difference between life and death. While such preparedness may be viewed negatively in our modern, instant-gratification society, recent global events, such as the pandemic, have awakened many to its significance.

PREPPERS IN THE OLD TESTAMENT

Indeed, Joseph's story in the Old Testament provides an example of prepping, though directed by God, during times of plenty to endure future hardship. As recounted in Genesis, Joseph interpreted Pharaoh's dreams as a warning of seven years of plenty followed by seven years of famine. With this foresight, Joseph advised Pharaoh to store surplus grain during the years of abundance to sustain the population during the ensuing famine. This prudent preparation not only saved Egypt from starvation but also provided sustenance to neighboring regions, including his father's (Jacob named Israel) family, ensuring their survival through the famine. Joseph's God-given wisdom and proactive measures serve as a timeless example of the importance of readiness and preparation for challenging times.

Prepping saved those from being killed in Jeremiah 41:8 who would of otherwise would have been killed during a time of war and famine. Proverbs 21:20 calls prepping a sign of a wise man.

But there were ten men among them who said to Ishmael, "Do not put us to death, for we have stores of wheat, barley, oil, and honey hidden in the fields." So he refrained and did not put them to death with their companions. (Jer. 41:8)

Precious treasure and oil are in a wise man's dwelling,
  but a foolish man devours it.
(Prov. 21:20)

COMFORT FOR BELIEVERS

For those feeling overwhelmed while reading this book, it is important to find comfort amidst the challenging scenarios discussed. Here are some reassuring points to consider:

1) Not all nations will submit: Despite the rise of the Antichrist's authority, it is crucial to remember that not all nations will yield to his rule. Scripture indicates that conflicts and wars will persist until the end (Dan. 9:26), suggesting that resistance to his authority will endure. Daniel 11:39 says this resistance will include the strongest fortresses. While this could entail physical attacks, it may also encompass other forms of disruption, such as restrictions on biblical represented goods like oil, grains, and wine. While these circumstances are difficult, individuals who have prepared may find themselves in a better position to weather such challenges.

2) Limited authority: The extent of the Antichrist's authority is not absolute. While it appears, he has absolute dominion over a quarter of the earth, it is unclear from Scripture whether this refers to geographical area or population. To mitigate persecution, individuals can consider avoiding regions directly under his control, especially those surrounding Israel, as suggested by passages like Ezekiel 30:5–6. Verse 3 calls it a day of Lord, which prophetically has not yet occurred.

> Cush, and Put, and Lud, and all Arabia, and Libya, and the people of the land that is in league, shall fall with them by the sword. "Thus says the Lord: Those who support Egypt shall fall. . . ." (Ezek. 30:5–6a)

> And after the sixty-two weeks, an anointed one shall be cut off and shall have nothing. And the people of the prince who is to come shall destroy the city and the sanctuary. Its end shall come with a flood, and to the end there shall be war. Desolations are decreed. (Dan. 9:26)

> And I looked, and behold, a pale horse! And its rider's name was Death, and Hades followed him. And they were *given authority over a fourth of the earth*, to kill with sword and with famine and with pestilence and by wild beasts of the earth. (Rev. 6:8, emphasis added)

3) Great tribulation cut short: Matthew 24:22 says that the great tribulation will be cut short. This means that its duration, during the second half of the seventieth week of Daniel, will not be as prolonged as initially anticipated. This divine intervention offers hope and relief to believers enduring tumultuous times.

4) The righteous will recognize false prophets: Despite the persecution, believers can take refuge knowing that when false prophets attempt to deceive them, as mentioned in Matthew 24:24–26, their attempts will ultimately fail, as indicated by Scripture's caveat "if possible."

> Then if anyone says to you, 'Look, here is the Christ!' or 'There he is!' do not believe it. For false christ's and false prophets will arise and perform great signs and wonders, so as to lead astray, *if possible*, even the elect. See, I have told you beforehand. So, if they say to you, 'Look, he is in the wilderness,' do not go out. If they say, 'Look, he is in the inner rooms,' do not believe it. (Matt. 24:23–26, emphasis added)

5) Hide during the fury: There is comfort in knowing when to hide during the intensified persecution period near the end of the great tribulation, referred to as the fury, which can provide solace. The duration of this fury is described as "a little while" (Isa. 26:20; John 14:19, 16:16–19; Rev. 6:11), allowing for some estimation.[1]

---

1 Chapter 12 of *Jesus's Return based on the Feasts of the Lord* provides guidance on this.

6) Mark of the beast: The inability to buy or sell without the mark of the beast (Rev. 13:16–17) underscores the need for endurance among believers (Rev. 14:12). This limitation on commerce necessitates preparation and readiness. Clues to the approaching great tribulation include awareness of the commencement of the seventieth week of Daniel (Dan. 9:27) and the ensuant opened seals outlined in Revelation 6:1–14 and parallel passages in the Olivet Discourse. Understanding these signs alerts believers when to prepare for the challenges ahead.

This preparation inevitably leads to a "prepper" mentality, whether individuals are consciously ready or not. Ensuring access to nourishment and medication becomes paramount for survival. Endurance becomes the overarching theme for believers being persecuted during the great tribulation with the anticipation of the blessed hope of the rapture (Titus 2:13). Revelation 12:13–16 depicts Israel, symbolized as a woman receiving nourishment, indicating God's provision even in the midst of tribulation.

7) Babylon betrayed diverts forces: Revelation 17:3 depicts a woman seated on a beast, identified as Babylon—the mother of prostitutes and abominations—in verse 5. There exists a symbiotic relationship between the woman and the beast, which is severed when the beast and its ten horns turn against her (Rev. 17:16). This betrayal will temporarily divert some of the military focus of the ten kings, potentially slowing down but not halting the persecution of Israel's offspring (the church), as Revelation 12:17 prophesies.

8) Jesus defends Israel at midpoint: Jesus's defensive battle in Jerusalem on Day 1 should be viewed as a counterattack against Gog and the coalition of ten kings as they initiated the attack (Ezek. 38). However, Jesus's retaliation will solely target the force attacking Israel, not the force targeting Babylon, as this aligns with God's will (Rev. 17:15–18). It is reasonable to expect that Jesus's selective response will initially impede the advancement of the great tribulation, albeit not halting it.

And the ten horns that you saw, they and the beast will hate the prostitute. They will make her desolate and naked, and devour her flesh and burn her up with fire, for *God has put it into their hearts to carry out his purpose* by being of one mind and handing over their royal power to the beast, until the words of God are fulfilled. (Rev. 17:16–17, emphasis added)

9) Mark of the beast: There is no explicit mention in Scripture, to the author's knowledge, that the mark of the beast is irremovable (Rev. 13:8, 12, 15; 14:9; 16:2; 20:4), unless it is coupled with worship of the beast and its image. Claims that taking the mark condemns one to Hades lack solid scriptural support and contradict the principle of free will. That is, some may incorrectly claim, someone else could commit one's soul to hell by holding them down against their will and give them the mark. However, it is not advisable to test this understanding by, for instance, using the mark to try and buy necessities for one's family.

10) Angel proclamations: Revelation 14:12 says that angels will proclaim the imperative to endure the great tribulation and to refuse the mark of the beast. However, wisdom dictates that we prepare beforehand. During this period described in the fifth opened seal, purchasing anything without the mark of the beast becomes impossible (Rev. 13:18–19). Scripture is likely hyperbole here since this beast will only have control over one fourth of the earth (Rev. 6:8). Those countries at war with these satanic ten kings (Dan. 9:26) would be expected to use a different form of currency, such as precious metals. Preparation includes essential items such as food, medicine, toiletries, water, fuel, and independence from municipal services.

Drawing a parallel from history, the Jewish people faced a similar plight after the destruction of Jerusalem by Babylon, as depicted in Lamentations 5:4. They had to purchase water and firewood for basic needs. Finding comfort in the knowledge of this impending persecution allows believers to prepare adequately for what lies ahead

> We must pay for the water we drink;
> the wood we get must be bought.
> (Lam. 5:4)

In times of uncertainty and distress, it is essential to hold onto these comforting truths and remain steadfast in faith. While the challenges may be daunting, believers can find solace in the promises of God and the hope of his ultimate deliverance.

CONCLUSION

The body of Christ is summoned to endure and have faith during the trials of the great tribulation, commencing at the midpoint of the seventieth week of Daniel. Most teachers and scholars do not teach this eschatological dual mandate (Rev. 13:10; 14:12). This period is characterized by the inability to engage in commerce without the satanic mark of the beast, emphasizing the necessity for prudent preparation among believers well in advance. The seven year covenant/treaty with many as prophesied in Daniel 9:27 will further debunk the pretribulation exegesis and affirm that the church and the Jewish people are indeed destined to persevere through the great tribulation of the fifth opened seal.

Chapter 12

Definitions

Antichrist: He represents the plural beast from the sea in Revelation 13:1–10 with ten horns (kingdoms) and seven heads. At the midpoint of the seventieth week, Satan (a spirit being) is expected to be thrown out of heaven (Rev. 12:7–12) and then indwell within the man of lawlessness. At that moment this one plural entity becomes the Antichrist. They are later separated in the seventh poured bowl when the man of lawlessness (a singular beast and human) is captured in Revelation 19:20 and Satan is captured in Revelation 20:1–3. Prior to the midpoint, the man of lawlessness should be called a prince, a singular beast, man of lawlessness, or an antichrist, though not the Antichrist. Figure 16 supports this plural Antichrist interpretation. Satan, a spirit being, has many names (dragon, serpent, devil) though scripturally is not considered the singular physical beast, that is only the man of lawlessness.

Apostasy: The apostasy must come before the 2 Thessalonians 2:1–4 day of the Lord. Hebrews 6:4–6 says they will "have tasted the heavenly gift, and have shared in the Holy Spirit," though they have fallen away. This eschatological falling away starts before the midpoint with its first day of the Lord. It occurs when they take the mark of beast and worship the demonic images as later proclaimed worldwide at the midpoint of the seventieth week with the third angel of Revelation 14:9–11. Disobeying this proclamation is eternity in hell, which there is no recourse, though still alive on earth. This irrevocable moment must be considered blasphemy against the Holy Spirit (Matt. 12:32).

Béma: *Strong's Concordance* defines the Greek noun *béma* (pronounced bay'- ma) as "a step, raised place" and, by implication, "a tribunal."[1] In Romans 14:10, it refers to the judgment seat of Christ: "We will all stand before the judgment seat of God; for it is written, 'As I live, says the Lord, every knee shall bow to me, and every tongue shall confess to God.' So then each of us will give an account of himself to God" (Rom. 14:10b–12).

---

1   James Strong, *Strong's Exhaustive Concordance of the Bible*, Bible Hub, s.v. "968 béma," accessed April 8, 2021, https://biblehub.com/greek/968. htm.

Revelation 11:18b describes this same event as "the time for the dead to be judged, and for rewarding your servants, the prophets and saints," which is part of the seventh blown trumpet. There are two judgments.

This is first where those who are raptured and resurrected (church and Israel) separately, now represent the bride, will stand before Christ individually to be judged. This will likely occur in Jerusalem. All those standing before Christ will have already been spiritually saved on earth. "For we must all appear before the judgment seat of Christ, so that each one may receive what is due for what he has done in the body, whether good or evil" (2 Cor. 5:10). This judgment is not for condemnation, but rather for rewards. Examples of being faithful include witnessing (Matt. 28:18–20), using your spiritual gifts (1 Cor. 12:1–11), and being victorious over sin (Rom. 6:1–4). The sheep, from the sheep and goat judgment, would not attend the béma for two reasons. Firstly, their rapture is based on works and not faith (Matt. 25:35–36). Secondly, they are not raptured until later (Rev. 16:18), likely during the seventh poured bowl. They would see the second judgment.

The second judgment is with the great white throne judgment in Revelation 20:11–15. This is after the millennium when the sheep of Matthew 25:31–46 (cf. Isa. 66:19–25) are reigned over for a thousand years. This is when the book of life is opened. Revelation 20:15 says, "And if anyone's name was not found written in the book of life, he was thrown into the lake of fire."

Beyond Prewrath: A premillennial view that Jesus returns, from heaven to earth, at the midpoint for a first gathering and a first day of the Lord, though not for an elect rapture. The church is raptured after the fifth opened seal of the great tribulation (Matt. 24:15–28; Rev. 6:9–11) evident with the Revelation 7:9–17 rejoicing in heaven. This specifically occurs in Revelation 8:5 with its unique theophany of "peals of thunder, rumblings, flashes of lightning (cf. Rev. 4:5 before the throne), and an earthquake" and a same day "day of the Lord" in Revelation 8:7 with its prophetic Luke 17:28–30 type of fire and death. The Revelation 7:9–17 rejoicing in the sky-heaven is seen as a consequence of this earthly rapture; that is, Revelation 6 to 8 chapters cannot be interpreted chronologically. The elect will not live through the entire second half of the seventieth week since the great tribulation will be cut short (Matt. 24:22), as evident with Matthew 24:29 and Revelation 6:12. To cut short does not change the duration of the second half of the seventieth week of 1,260 days, it will simply lengthen the seven blown trumpet judgments.

Israel is later raptured at the end of the seventieth week in Revelation 11:19 with its same great dispensational theophany fulfilling their seventy prophetic weeks (Dan. 9:24–25). The bride of Christ, who are the church and Israel, then attend the béma in Revelation 11:18. The last rapture theophany in Revelation 16:18 is for the Matthew 25:35–36 works-based sheep who attend the marriage supper as wedding guests and later become the subjects ruled over during the millennium.

Bride of Christ: They represent both the church and Israel who arrive separately from a different chronological rapture and resurrection (Rev. 8:5 during the seventh opened seal; 11:19 during the seventh blown trumpet, and 1 Thess. 3:13 resurrection at the midpoint).

Christ, Marriage of: The concept of the marriage of Christ in Jewish tradition commences with the betrothal, followed by the marriage and consummation. The initial betrothal occurred when the Jewish people were united with God in Exodus 19–20 on Mt. Sinai. This union was later dissolved with the crucifixion of Jesus, seen as the bridegroom. A subsequent second betrothal is considered to have taken place with the resurrection of Jesus and the sending and receiving of the Holy Spirit. This second union is inclusive of both Jew and Gentile, spanning across past, present, and future, as indicated in Ephesians 3:6 (cf. Isa. 56:1–8) where the church is depicted as part of the bride. Scripture reveals, "The mystery is that the Gentiles are fellow heirs, members of the same body, and partakers of the promise in Christ Jesus through the gospel." The culmination of the wedding ceremony for the bride of Christ is depicted later in Revelation 19:7–8 when the bride is adorned in pure, fine linen. The consummation of this marriage occurs as they live together on earth during Jesus's millennial reign.

Christ, Marriage Supper of: The marriage supper of the Lord is with the bride of Christ (church and Jewish people) and Jesus. It occurs after the marriage in Revelation 19:9–10. The guests of Matthew 22:1–10 would attend the marriage feast. The guests are identified as the works-based sheep (Matt. 25:35–36) from the sheep and goat judgment.

Cut short: Matthew 24:22 relates to the duration of the great tribulation duration being reduced when it starts at the middle of the seventieth week. If it was not cut short, the maximum duration would be less than 1,110 days (1,260 days minus five months of the fifth blown trumpet). This is a different event, though it chronologically overlaps, than 2 Thessalonians 1:7 when relief of three and half years (Rev. 12:13–16) is given to only the Jewish remnant who flee (Zech. 14:5; Matt. 24:15–20) to the east, which has chronological parallels to 2 Thessalonians 2:1–4 at the midpoint.

Day of Christ (rapture), eschatological: Relates to being physically separated from persecution with rewards and blessings. The rewards and blessings are different for the faith-based bride of Christ (church and Israel) and the works-based sheep. The bride of Christ will attend the béma for eternal rewards. The sheep are separated during the sheep and goat judgment of Matthew 25:31–46 to inherit the millennial kingdom when Jesus reigns on earth.

Day of the Lord, eschatological: Relates to the Lord's judgment against the wicked. A day of the Lord is always considered with the presence of Jesus Christ. This can also include others from heaven, such as angels or the army of God. It can occur while the righteous are still living on the earth; that is, it can be targeted against the wicked in Israel, just as it was with Lot (Gen. 19:14–29) and the Jewish people who were in Egyptian exile (Ex. 8:22). One eschatological example of this targeting is with Zechariah 14:1; a day of the LORD targeted against the wicked attacking Israel, and at that same moment, the church and Israel enter the great tribulation and Jacob's trouble.

There are seven proposed eschatological days of the Lord. A day of the Lord always includes Jesus in the fighting force. If God is not present, then it is considered the wrath of God. For example, a wrath of God would be the angel's fifth blown trumpet, when there are apocalyptic locusts from the bottomless pit.

Day of the Lord (first): This is the first of three battles of Jesus called the Jerusalem battle. It is when the second return of Jesus begins with a day of the Lord and a gathering with Jesus, and the return of Satan with a great tribulation and Jacob's trouble, which all begin at the midpoint. This is a time of persecution unparallelled in all of the history of persecution. A few Scriptures which support this include: Jeremiah 30:7; Daniel 12:1; Matthew 24:15, 21; Daniel 9:27; and Zechariah 14:1. The church rapture does not occur until after the great tribulation.

Darkness: Unless noted otherwise, this is defined as at least one twenty-four-hour cycle of eschatological darkness. The definition helps to simply the author's graphs. Darkness appears to be during the following five events: part of Day 1 (Zech. 14:6–7), sixth opened seal (Rev. 6:12), fifth blown trumpet (Rev. 9:2), part of the sixth blown trumpet (Rev. 14:17–19, cf. Acts 2:17–21), and fifth poured bowl (Rev. 16:10). There are likely two more unidentified darkness events since that would make seven a number which is prevalent in eschatology.

Dispensation: Historically, this has been defined as how God's plans are distinguished between the church (Gentiles) and Israel (Jews).

Elect: The elect must live through the great tribulation of Matthew 24:15–28 (cf. Rev. 7:9–17). Their persecution is "cut short" with the opening of the sixth seal in Revelation 6:12 and parallel of Matthew 24:29. The elect is later raptured during the opening of the seventh seal of specifically Revelation 8:5. The Jewish people must live through the last entire seventieth week in Daniel 9:24 before they can be raptured during the seventh blown trumpet of Revelation 11:19. After both faith–based groups are raptured, they will attend the béma in Revelation 11:18, likely in Jerusalem.

Endure: Scripture requires the righteous to eschatologically endure (Rev. 14:12). To endure is to keep the first (vv. 6–7) and third (vv. 9–11) angel proclamations, which are given at or moments before the midpoint. Enduring should not be considered actions taken to earn spiritual salvation as some claim with their misinterpretation of Matthew 10:22, which says, "And you will be hated by all for my name's sake. But the one who endures to the end will be saved."

Salvation is a free gift, which cannot be earned (Eph. 2:8–9), though only by calling on the name of the Lord (Rom. 6:23; 10:9–13). The saints not enduring (Rev. 14:12) should be considered disobeying the third angel proclamation of taking the mark of the beast and worshiping the demonic beings (Rev. 14:9–11). Once someone falls away (2 Thess. 2:3), a strong delusion is sent by God (2 Thess. 2:11–12), which prevents them from later repenting. This eternal unforgivable sin of the third angel, while still alive on earth, must be considered blasphemy of the Holy Spirit (Matt. 12:32) since there is no other interpretation. All other sins are Scripturally forgivable with Jesus through repentance, while still alive on earth. When we are eschatologically persecuted, we are to have both physical endurance and spiritual faith (Rev. 13:10; 14:12).

Eschatology: A branch of theology concerned with future biblical end–time prophecy fulfillment, including, for example, Jesus's second coming, His thousand-year reign on earth, and then a new earth and heaven.

False Prophet: He represents the beast from the earth in Revelation 13. He performs great signs (v. 13), deceives those on the earth (v. 14), and was allowed to give breath to the image of the beast (v. 15).

Fury: Near the end of the great tribulation, the persecution tempo (fury) will increase and then end abruptly (Isa. 26:20; Matt. 24:29; Rev. 6:11–12). This increased persecution is when we are to hide in our chambers (rooms of our houses) for "a little while."

Gather to him (2 Thess. 2:1): 2 Thessalonians 2:1 says "Our being gathered (Greek *episynagōgēs*) to him" which is when Jesus is on or approaching the Mt. of Olives in Zechariah 14:4 and those in Jerusalem on their housetops in Matthew 24:17. This occurs at the midpoint the same day of Jesus's (Matt. 24:27) and Satan's (Isa. 14:12; Rev. 12:7–12) parousia from heaven to earth. This first gathering cannot be representative of a rapture since the church and Israel must now live through the fifth opened seal with its great tribulation. Therefore, at least two gatherings must be deduced since there is a later gathering in the sky (Matt. 24:30–31) as a consequence of the elect rapture. A total of seven eschatological gatherings are proposed in beyond prewrath view.

Gather his elect (Matt. 24:31): The Matthew 24:31 *angels gather his elect* (Greek *episynaxousin*), and they meet Jesus in the sky (Matt. 24:30; 1 Thess. 4:17; Rev. 1:7), is representative of the consequence of the elect rapture. This occurs after the great tribulation, though before the first trumpet judgment.

Grant relief: The Jewish remnant who follow the Old Testament directions of Zechariah 14:5 to flee toward the valley of my mountains will be granted persecution relief (2 Thess. 1:7) during the second half of the seventieth week of Daniel (Rev. 12:14). This is at the midpoint when their prayers are interrupted, and they go to their Jerusalem housetops (Isa. 22:1) to see Jesus nearby on the Mt. of Olives in his majesty. This is the first gathering. Moments later they flee in an eastward direction (Matt. 24:17), possibly to the Dead Sea salt caverns taken by new temple flowing water.

Great dispensational theophanies: In general, a theophany is a visible manifestation to humankind of God or a god. There are only three scriptural unique great dispensational theophanies of "peals of thunder, rumblings, flashes of lightning, and an earthquake," which are located in Revelation 8:5, 11:19, and 16:18. Each is reflective of a unique earthly rapture. This is defined as first for the church (Gentiles), second mainly for Israel (Jews), and last for the *sheep*. The *sheep* are reflective of the sheep and goat judgment in Matthew 25:31–46 where they will inherit the millennial kingdom, will be reigned over, live long lives, though they (this first generation) are expected to have a physical death before the thousand years are complete. The same theophany can be found in Revelation 4:5 without the earthquake. Verses 4–11 identifies the source of this same unique theophany, without the earthquake, as the Lord God who sits on the throne. These divine theophanies are distinct in their use of thunder and lightning, which is almost always associated with the righteous, each symbolizing a rapture event.

Great tribulation: The great tribulation is placed during the fifth opened seal, which starts with the abomination of desolation at the midpoint (Matt. 24:15). It is an unparalleled time of persecution on the earth "so great there is none is like it" (Jer. 30:7). The persecution is so great that no one will be able to buy or sell without the satanic mark of beast. Matthew 24:21–22 says that the persecution will be cut short for the elect. The great tribulation could appropriately be called the Antichrist's great tribulation since it begins when Satan is thrown down to earth from heaven and pursues the woman (Israel), though this remnant is nourished for 1,260 days. On the day that Satan is thrown out of heaven, he indwells within the man of lawlessness (beast), and there is an abomination of desolation at the Jewish temple at the midpoint.

Harpazó (rapture): A Greek verb meaning to carry off by force or snatch away. It occurs fourteen times in the New Testiment.[2] The original Latin translation used *rapio*, which is where we get the English word rapture. Depending on the context, it means to be taken away to another location on earth or else to heaven. One example of a horizontal rapture is the apostle Philip who after he baptized the eunuch in Acts 8:39 was taken away to another location on the earth.

Heaven: There are three types of heaven. The first is the sky where Jesus ascended to in Acts 1:11. The second is outer space or stars. The third is God's throne.

---

2   Matt. 11:12; 12:29; 13:19; John 6:15; 10:12, 28, 29; Acts 8:39; 23:10; 2 Cor. 12:2, 4; 1 Thess. 4:17; Jude 1:23; Rev. 12:5.

Jacob's trouble, time of: This begins at the midpoint with the fifth opened seal of the great tribulation. This time of persecution on earth is unparalleled in human history (Jer. 30:7; Dan. 12:1; Matt. 24:21). It ends when the sixth seal is opened, and the tribulation ends. The latter sixth blown trumpet is shown to have idols (Rev. 9:20), which means the persecution would likely start up again in the trumpet judgments.

Therefore, a case can be made that the Jewish people's troubles resume during the blown trumpets, though not to the extreme persecution of the fifth opened seal. Scripture identifies a group of Jewish people, the woman of Revelation 12:15, being protected and nourished during these trumpet judgments of God. There is another group of 144,000, from the twelve Hebrew tribes, who arrive on earth and are sealed in Revelation 7 before these trumpet judgments. Zechariah 13:7–9a generally describes Israel living through persecution. All of the Jewish people who are spiritually saved in Acts 2:21 (cf. Zech. 13:9b) during the sixth blown trumpet will be physically resurrected and raptured later during the seventh blown trumpet in Revelation 11:19 when their decreed seventieth prophetic week is completed in Daniel 9:24.

Jesus's return: It will begin in the middle of the seventieth week of Daniel when Jesus returns the way he left (Acts 1:9–11; cf. Matt. 24:27). That day will include a gathering (Matt. 24:17; 2 Thess. 2:1) and day of the Lord (Zech. 14:1, 5; 2 Thess. 2:1–4). Jesus's return extends into the millennium when he reigns from Jerusalem for one thousand years. This is not a midtribulation rapture since it is not at the midpoint though the elect rapture is after the fifth opened seal great tribulation.

Numbers, Eschatological:

> One Antichrist: Comes into existence at the midpoint when Satan, a spirit being, enters the man of lawlessness. This is a reflection of when Satan entered the man of Judas Iscariot.

> One Béma: One for the bride of Christ, both the church and Israel.

> One wedding supper: Attended by the bride of Christ (church and Israel) and the guests (works-based sheep) from the sheep and goat judgment.

Two parousias: One for Jesus and one for Satan, both leaving heaven and arriving on earth at the midpoint of the seventieth week.

Two, possibly three, chronological pairs of gatherings and same day "day of the Lord."

Three battles of Jesus: Jerusalem, Jehoshaphat, and Armageddon.

Three raptures: Church, Israel, and the works-based sheep.

Seven: See septets definition.

Olivet Discourse: The Olivet Discourse is coined as representing the eschatological teaching given by Jesus Christ on the Mt. of Olives. This discourse is recorded in the synoptic gospels of Matthew 24:1–25:46, Mark 13:1–37, and Luke 21:5–36. They have chronological parallels with Revelation 6 and 8.

Parousia: Parousia is defined in *Strong's Concordance* as a Greek noun "a presence" or "a coming," though not necessarily limited to the return of Christ. The concordance says it is a "technical term with reference to the visit of a king or some other official, 'a royal visit.'"[3] It can have either a blessing or a judgment component. One parousia example of a negative sense is Satan with the help of the man of lawlessness in 2 Thessalonians 2:9. Both Jesus's and Satan's parousia, from heaven to earth, are at the midpoint. Jesus likely arrives on earth just before Satan since Jesus is not in the Revelation 12:7–12 heavenly battle.

Pretribulation: Pretribulation refers to the belief that the rapture of the church has been imminent since Jesus ascended into heaven in Acts 1, without requiring any preceding event. Proponents of this view suggest that the church's rapture will coincide with the apostle John's vision of being caught up to heaven in Revelation 4:1, although there is no specific mention of rejoicing in heaven comparable to the celebration described for their "tribulation saints" in Revelation 7:9–17. According to this view, the rapture

---

3   James Strong, *Strong's Exhaustive Concordance of the Bible*, Bible Hub, s.v. "3952 parousia," accessed September 8, 2023, https://biblehub.com/greek/3952.htm.

will take place before the start of the seventieth week of Daniel described in Revelation 6:1, which begins with the opening of the first seal.

Adherents of the pretribulation view describe the rapture as a secret event. This is in contrast to Scripture (1 Thess. 4:17; Rev. 1:7) that says every eye will see Jesus. They maintain that Jesus's second coming will occur later on a white horse with the battle of Armageddon.

Prewrath Rapture: A premillennial rapture of the church and the return of Christ, from heaven to earth, occur concurrently. The elect (church) will be raptured after the great tribulation though before the same-day day of the Lord starting in Revelation 8:1. The Antichrist persecution starts at the midpoint of the seventieth week of Daniel. The elect persecution will be cut short, reducing the great tribulation duration of the fifth opened seal within the second half of the seventieth week.

Restrainer: The restrainer is the archangel Michael. Satan and his angel's heavenly restraint release date is proposed to occur at the midpoint. Michael standing up in Daniel 12:1 is considered a metaphor to when he takes the lead to authorize God's angels to release their restraints. This then seems to begin the battle in heaven. God's righteous angels have a two to one numerical advantage and will overcome the rebellious angels and then throw them to earth as described in Revelation 12:7–12. This is Satan's parousia, from heaven to earth, in Luke 10:18.

Since Jesus in not mentioned in the heavenly battle, there is support that Jesus's parousia to the Mt. of Olives (Zech. 14:4) was before their restraints were released, at the midpoint with its same day abomination of desolation at the Jerusalem temple. The release of their restraints seems to be timed to the exact midpoint of when the fifth opened seal of the great tribulation begins. This is representative of "Your (the Father's) will being done...in heaven" by His angels (Matt. 6:10).

Resurrection, first: The Second Coming of Jesus—from heaven to earth—is described in Scripture as occurring "with all His saints" (1 Thess. 3:13), indicating a concurrent event. His coming is proposed to take place at the midpoint (start of the great tribulation with the fifth seal), which appears to chronologically align with a resurrection of the dead (Dan. 12:2; 1 Cor. 15:52). Note, Daniel 12:1 describes a time of trouble for the Jewish people living, deduced to be the midpoint great tribulation (cf. Dan. 9:27; Matt. 24:15; Rev. 12:14). According to the beyond prewrath dispensational understanding, the rapture of the elect (Matt. 24:30–31; 1 Thess. 4:17–18;

Rev. 8:5) is associated with the seventh seal, suggesting that a resurrection occurs earlier in the prophetic timeline.

Nowhere in Scripture is it explicitly stated that the resurrection and the elect rapture happen on the same day, as some premillennial proponents claim. Rather, 1 Thessalonians 4:13–18 simply requires that the resurrection precedes the catching up of the living.

Another resurrection appears to be suggested in Revelation 6:9–11, where the opening of the fifth seal reveals the souls of the martyred under the altar, clothed in white robes—an indication of physical bodies. This implies that their resurrection occurs after the midpoint first resurrection. The mention of their fellow servants and brothers who are yet to be killed further suggests an additional resurrection. From a dispensational perspective, a subsequent resurrection seems to include any of the elect who die—regardless of the cause—after the midpoint first resurrection, continuing until the rapture of the elect described in Revelation 8:5 therefore fulfilling 1 Thessalonians 4:13–18 resurrection before the rapture.

Salvation: Salvation is based on grace alone through faith alone in Christ alone. It cannot be earned.

Second coming of Christ: Jesus's first coming was a series of chronological events, that is his conception, birth, spiritual growth prior to ministry, ministry of at least three years, crucifixion, resurrection, and ascension into heaven. In a similar way, Jesus's second coming should also be considered a series of chronological events. It starts at the midpoint with a gathering as described in chapter 1, though not for a rapture. There are seven eschatological days of the Lord (against the wicked) and three days of Christ (rapture for faith-based church, faith-based Israel, and works-based sheep). The second coming of Christ can be viewed as extending into the millennium when Jesus reigns for a thousand years and into eternity for the new earth and heavens.

Septet: A septet is a group of seven similar things. In reference to eschatology: seven lamp stands—churches—stars (Rev. 1–3), seven days of the Lord, seven thunders (Rev. 10:3), seven earthquakes, seven opened seals, seven blown trumpets, and seven poured bowls. Seven gatherings are proposed. Seven earthquakes were proposed in *Beyond Prewrath End-Time Prophecy* chapter 6.

Sheep and Goat Judgment: Matthew 25:31–46 distinguishes between the sheep, who are described as "blessed by my Father (v. 34)," and the goats, who are "cursed into the eternal fire (v. 41)." Verses 35–36 outline six actions that characterize someone as a sheep. Additionally, they must have obeyed the third angel's proclamation of Revelation 14:9–11, though they never accepted the eternal gospel by repenting of their sins as outlined in the first angel's proclamation (Rev. 14:6–7). This obedience ensures that when the third great dispensational theophany occurs in Revelation 16:18, during the pouring out of the seventh bowl, they will be raptured. Since their rapture is based on works rather than on faith, they will eventually, after a long life, experience physical death after inheriting their millennial kingdom. As described in Matthew 19:28 and Revelation 20:4–5, they must be deduced as the subjects ruled over during this period.

Tribulation: This begins during the fourth opened seal (Matt. 24:9–14; Rev. 6:7–8) followed by the fifth seal with a great tribulation (Matt. 24:15–26; Rev. 6:9–11). The persecution ends when the sixth seal is opened (Matt. 24:29; Rev. 6:12–17), which is when those who are being persecuted for their faith can rejoice. Tribulation cannot be used as a label to represent the seventieth week of Daniel since the sixth opened seal, within the seventieth week, explicitly says that seal does not have tribulation.

Wrath of God: The eschatological wrath of God is against the wicked, with or without Jesus Christ presence. Most premillennial views have only one eschatological generic wrath of God. Beyond prewrath has four. The first is at the midpoint in Zechariah 14:1 with a day of the Lord. The second is during the sixth seal with the wrath of the Lamb in Revelation 6:12–17, which represents being humbled with its parallel Isaiah 2:10–12. The third wrath of God is the seven blown trumpets and seven poured bowls. The fourth is fifteen months after the beast was killed in the seventh poured bowl (Dan. 7:12; Rev. 19:20). Sometimes the wrath of God includes angels, within the blown trumpets and the poured bowls. The fifth trumpet is unique in that it has an attacking force of apocalyptic locusts coming from the bottomless pit. Armageddon in the seventh poured bowl would include the armies of heaven. So, the eschatological wrath of God attacking force could come from heaven (Jesus, angels, or heavenly saints) or hell with their apocalyptic locusts.

Subject Index

Scripture Index

Revelation (*continued*)

Previous books by Robert Parker

Beyond Prewrath End-Time Prophecy

Jesus's Return Based on the Feasts of the Lord
